HUN✦ING
F O R GOD

Encountering the Sacred in the Great Outdoors

FISHING
F O R THE LORD

HUNING
_F_O_R GOD

Encountering the Sacred in the Great Outdoors

FISHING
_F^{THE}_O_R LORD

REV. JOSEPH F. CLASSEN

Our Sunday Visitor Publishing Division
Our Sunday Visitor, Inc.
Huntington, Indiana 46750

Copyright © 2006 by Our Sunday Visitor Publishing Division
Our Sunday Visitor, Inc.   Published 2006
14 13 12 11 10   2 3 4 5 6

Our Sunday Visitor Publishing Division
Our Sunday Visitor, Inc.
200 Noll Plaza
Huntington, IN 46750

ISBN-13: 978-1-59276-217-0
ISBN-10: 1-59276-217-4 (Inventory No. T268)
LCCN: 2006930757

Cover design by Troy Lefevra
Interior design by Sherri L. Hoffman
Cover photos courtesy of Brand X, Photodisc, and DesignPics
Interior photos provided by the author

PRINTED IN THE UNITED STATES OF AMERICA

Contents

The error of creating one's own "religion." True spirituality and the Holy Spirit. Discerning the work of the Spirit.

As a deer longs for flowing streams,
so my soul longs for you, O God.

— PSALM 42:1 (NRSV)

Rev. Joseph F. Classen with his parents

Acknowledgments

FIRST OF ALL, thanks be to God (What else did you expect from a priest?) for filling my soul with a passionate love for the wonders of His creation and for the many opportunities to experience His presence in the great outdoors. I'd like to thank my Dad for planting the initial seed that brought about such a love of the natural world and of the God who decided that it should be. Thanks, of course, to my Mom and all of my family for their love and support.

I'd like to thank and salute all my friends (more like brothers, really) with whom I have shared so many great outdoor experiences over the years. Here's to many more!

I'd like to thank all those great people who have allowed me to spend time on their farms and property. These have been the places that a good deal of my hunting for God and fishing for the Lord has taken place. Words cannot describe how grateful I am to all of you.

I'd like to thank all the wise and thoughtful teachers, theologians, philosophers, and writers who have influenced me over the years and who have helped fashion the lens through which I see the world.

I'd like to thank the countless people out there who I have crossed paths with at one time or another. You've inspired me in ways you'll never realize.

Last, but certainly not least, I'd like to offer my deepest and sincerest appreciation and gratitude to everybody at OSV for believing in this project and making it a reality.

God bless all of you!

FR. JOE CLASSEN

11

CHAPTER 1

Introduction:
"Do Something Constructive!"

IT WAS JANUARY 16, 2004. The bow-hunting season had successfully come to an end and I found myself in the woods for no other reason than to simply be there. It was the first time in months that I took to the timber while not sleep-deprived and without strained eyes from an overtaxed concentration or a slight headache from forced mental hyper-alertness. I was totally rested. I was delightfully refreshed. It was a long-forgotten joy to simply stroll through the woods with no fear of the consequences of spooking game or starting off that chain reaction of wildlife intruder alert.

With every leaf that crunched under my now carefree heavy footsteps, I felt a growing sense of rejuvenation. As I watched the steam of my breath mingle and disappear into the crisp winter air, I decided to sit down on the stump of a freshly cut oak. I couldn't remember the last time that I felt so filled with peace. As I became mesmerized by the melodically repetitious sounds of the Missouri songbirds, I began to wonder if the stillness could stop time. It was then that the realization of what I was experiencing hit me. It had come full circle. I had finally recaptured the purity and blessedness with which I experienced God through nature as a child.

As I continued to rest upon the remains of the fallen giant of a tree, I had the initial inspiration to write this book. And so I began to ask myself, "Where do I begin? How does one start to write a book about so many experiences and so many lessons learned? What is the purpose of such a book? Why should I even attempt to write it? After all, I'm not a noted author, and with regard to the outdoors, I've never caught a world-record fish or taken a record-book animal. What do I have to offer the reader? There have been lots of books written about hunting and fishing techniques and stories of remarkable outdoor adventures. There are volumes written on humorous mishaps and philosophical insights in regards to hunting and fishing. Where will I fit in?"

Those were just some of the questions that plagued me as I began to consider this project. Most of all, I was initially a bit nervous about what people may think about me writing such a book. I didn't want to come off as some sort of egomaniac who's written a book in praise of himself, glorifying all the things he's done, or as a priest who has his priorities terribly confused.

As these matters continued to trouble me, I thought back to my first year of college. On one occasion I attended an open-mike night where students and some faculty read their short stories and poems to the curious folks in attendance. I remember watching how the presenters would rather pompously stroll up to the microphone and deliver their "art," which was usually filth-ridden stories about their devious sexual exploits or a poem reflecting some nonsensical drug induced banter. After dumping their intellectual garbage into the ears of the listeners, they'd defiantly strut back to their places, filled with arrogance as if their work had unlocked the very mysteries of life and death.

Needless to say, that's not me. This book is not an exercise in egoism or a pathetic act of self-glorification. If anything, it's about being humbled. This book is not a pat on the back for significant outdoor achievements; in fact, the heart and true purpose of this book really have nothing to do with the outdoors at all. As the reader will soon discover, the pursuits of fishing and hunting have been a sacred catalyst which has revealed and guided me to something profoundly more significant than merely catching fish and harvesting game. This book is about the realization of the divine, about self discovery, and about spiritual and personal growth. It is a vehicle for the Gospel message of Jesus Christ. It is an opportunity to pass on and share some unique insights and experiences of God working in and through the great outdoors. These experiences have taught me many valuable life lessons, have built character, and have helped me to develop virtue. They've taught me to appreciate many things that I've taken for granted. Most of all, they've renewed my soul and healed me in times when I've felt utterly broken.

Of course, the next big question is, "Hey, you're a priest, when do you have time to do all this hunting and fishing, much less write a book?" To answer that, I'd like to quote my mother, who always said, "Do something constructive!" As a kid, if ever my mom caught my brother and me being lazy bums and just sitting around watching TV for long periods of time, she'd turn off the TV and tell us to do something more constructive. That usually meant going outside to play or doing an activity that actually involved the use of the brain.

Her motto has always stuck with me. Throughout the years I've found that I am really not much of a TV guy. I watch a few shows here and there and a movie now and again, but because of that parental directive to do something more "constructive," I have always preferred to spend free time doing something that involved a good measure of creativity. And so to answer the question: Like anyone, I do have some down time, days off, and vacation time. When I have a free hour here or there, I use that time doing something like praying, playing guitar, exercising, reading, writing, tying flies, practicing archery, et cetera. Most of my seemingly big, non-parish related activities (like writing a book) are the result of work being done in very small bits and pieces. It's time that most people would have spent sitting (rotting) in front of the TV.

As far as having time to hunt and fish, I have one day off a week and a few weeks of vacation each year. And you can bet that during that time I'll be in the woods or on the water. It's not necessarily the quantity of time that produces success in the ways of fishing and hunting. It's well-planned, skillfully prepared, and carefully executed *quality* of time that counts. And, of course, the main ingredient is always to offer that time to the Lord. When you go fishing or hunting with God, you'll always catch something big — though maybe not a fish — and you'll always harvest something of trophy quality — though maybe not an animal.

Throughout this book the reader will discover, time and time again, that fishing is not just about catching a fish and hunting is not just about harvesting game. In much the same way, gardening is not just about growing things, and working on cars is not just about changing your oil or putting on new brakes. There's something else far more important going on.

Let me explain this phenomenon. I once was in an art class where the instructor had us spend an hour drawing a piece of popcorn. But before we began, he asked us to be aware of what we were thinking about while drawing. Before class was over, we spent some time discussing what we'd each thought about while doing this seemingly mundane task of drawing popcorn. It was amazing to hear what everyone was thinking about. Some people were engaged in thoughts of problem solving. Others were thinking about friends and family. Each person was thinking about something different, but all of us were *thinking* about something. We were aware of our awareness, which is one of the things that makes us uniquely human.

So many things in our present culture are devoid of any real thought or reflection. The sedentary lifestyle many of us can end up living at times sucks dry the true potential we all have as human beings. We watch the events of someone else's life on TV, someone who isn't even real. We spend hours watching someone else play a game — we even consider ourselves part of the team — and yet we never get off the couch to get some exercise for ourselves. Popular music that we may (or may not) listen to is filled with lyrics about basically nothing. By means of mass-media advertising, we're told what to wear, what to eat, what to drive, where to live, how to be "politically correct," what moral beliefs to adhere to, and what new gadgets we must have to make our busy lives more manageable. Our possessions come to possess us. Our culture thinks for us, feels for us, and manipulates us in ways we hardly give much thought to. And that's because we hardly have a chance to give it much thought. Our culture can turn us into thoughtless, spineless fools if we give it the chance.

Thus, the vital importance of constructive activities emerges. We have to give ourselves a chance to think. And just like drawing that piece of popcorn, when we engage in activities that gently occupy the body and the senses, the soul is free to be refreshed and nourished. Our intellect is set free to think on its own. Our will is able to be strengthened. And what better place to do that than the great outdoors! (Besides coming to Church, of course!)

Having a fishing rod, a walking stick, or a gun/bow in hand is simply a doorway to the true refreshment that comes from being immersed in the beauty of God's creation. While catching a nice fish or harvesting that big ol' buck is the icing on the cake, there are still many lessons one learns while trying to eat that cake.

CHAPTER 2

The Need for Nature

AFTER THE TRAGIC EVENTS of September 11, 2001, there was a noted spiritual re-awakening all across the nation. People who hadn't been to church in a long time began going back. Others began attending church for the first time. But even before that horrible day, there has been a steadily growing interest in spiritual awareness. People have been searching for some kind of manifestation of God in their lives with great enthusiasm, and people are finding it in different ways. Though most folks seek the spiritual in mainstream churches and religions, many have looked in other areas such as "new age" religions or even in areas related to the occult. Upon further study, one will find that most of these "new age" spiritualities are basically revitalized pagan practices of centuries ago. In the majority of these spiritualities, the manifestation of God is sought and experienced in things like nature, astrology, geology, and things that directly and primarily affect the senses.

As St. Paul pointed out to the early Christian communities, yes, God is manifest in all of creation. There is no doubt that we experience the manifestation of God in things like the beauty of nature and the wonder of all created things, but it shouldn't stop there. All creation points to the creator, and it is God who is to be the object of our worship. As Christians, we rejoice because the

God who is made manifest in all of creation has taken on human flesh and was born of the Virgin Mary. We rejoice because we don't have to look for God in things like trees, the earth, the four winds, fire, crystals, animals, and so forth. God has manifested himself to us in the person of Jesus Christ — a man who walked, talked, healed the sick, forgave sinners, suffered and died on the cross for our sake, rose again from the dead, and purchased for us salvation and eternal life.

So often we expect God to manifest himself in ways that dazzle us and in ways that would be so profound that there would be no doubt left in our minds as to his existence. We want God to entertain us and zap us with his power and wisdom. Like those caught up in these "new age" practices, we often want God to manifest himself in ways that we can see, touch, smell, and experience with all of our senses.

With time, we find out that this usually is not how God works in our lives. The old saying holds true: "God works in mysterious ways." God generally works in our lives through ordinary means, which have extraordinary results. However, it can only be perceived through the eyes of faith. Being that we as human beings are made in the image and likeness of God, we experience God most profoundly through one another. I don't know how many times I've had prayers answered by means of a totally out-of-the-blue phone call, email, letter, or conversation with someone. There have been times when an encounter with a complete stranger turned out to be a moment of true divine intervention. God is active in our lives every day, yet we so often fail to recognize that because we're still looking for God in all the wrong places.

And so the question remains, what role does nature play in one's Christian faith? Is there a need for nature in our spiritual lives? As stated earlier, there is a real danger in focusing our attention too much on creation instead of the Creator. Another danger is the unrealistic view of what I like to call the "nature of nature." In our present day many of us have greatly disconnected ourselves from the reality of what goes on in nature. We like to think that things happen in nature just like in a Disney movie. This "Bambi syndrome," as my dad likes to call it, has significantly clouded the objective truth of the matter. The nature of nature is that of indifference to life and death. The food chain, which we are a part of, is very real. With even the slightest bit of objective study, one will find that animals spend every day of their lives doing one thing: surviving. Their mission in life is to eat, avoid danger, and propagate the species (at certain times of the year). There is very little, if any, romance or chivalry in nature. The law of the jungle has not changed. With a bit more objective study, one will observe the undeniable fact that animals are far more brutal and savage to one another than any human could ever imagine (unless they are extremely disturbed).

A mountain lion will never become a vegetarian because it feels bad about killing a lamb. A large mouth bass will never start chowing down on moss and weeds because he's remorseful about all the other fish he's killed and eaten. A whitetail buck doesn't shed a tear over brutalizing and sometimes even killing a less dominant buck during the rut. Male bears will attempt to kill their own offspring just so they can breed with the mothers again. I've seen a photographic documentary where a pack of coyotes kill a yearling doe by first chewing its face off, then ripping the flesh off its legs, and finally several minutes later killing it (sorry for the graphic details, but that's the reality). My dad's cat used to catch rabbits and spend the afternoon basically torturing the poor things to death. Are these animals evil? No. They are simply acting in accordance with the nature of their nature. When a hunter kills a deer or any game animal, it's quick and clean. Any serious hunter insists on it. Though sometimes very sick human beings do dreadful things that only a savage beast would do, thank God our nature is not that of an animal.

Another disturbing trend that comes from our misguided sense of nature is that we often do treat animals with more respect, concern, and genuine love than we do our fellow man. As the stewards of creation (according to Genesis), it is our God-given duty and responsibility to take care of, and treat with respect, all of our resources and all the gifts God has given us, including animals. With that being said, however, it's quite disturbing when married couples purposely avoid having a child, or worse yet, have an abortion and instead desire to become "pet parents." Something's gone seriously wrong when we'd rather make a significant financial donation to help a stray dog or cat than to help a homeless human being. When we'd rather buy Christmas gifts for an animal instead of for a neighbor who'll have none, we've certainly gone down the wrong path.

Many misguided "animal rights" organizations raise lots of money from donations each year, while organizations that deal with human beings often go broke and scratch to make ends meet. As a fellow priest once pointed out, "The greatest gift we have to offer anyone is our love, and how often we 'throw our pearls before swine' (see Mt 7:6) instead of first offering it to one another, who are made in the image and likeness of God."

We hear a lot about being "humane" these days. It's interesting to note that being "humane" means to be concerned with the alleviation of suffering and to display evidence of moral and intellectual advancement. With that being said, having more concern for a starving puppy (while still a noble and valid concern), and at the same time turning our backs on the starving people in our own neighborhoods, is not a sign of moral and intellectual advancement. It's a sign of severely irresponsible moral priority and intellectual degeneration.

Nonetheless, the undeniable fact of the matter is that we do experience something in nature and in animals that is not savage, but beautiful. We experience tranquillity in the midst of often unseen chaos. Spending time in the natural world does something very positive to us. We see in animals and in our pets qualities that we often don't see, or usually fail to see, in one another. As we sit in the predawn darkness and watch the sun come up and the world come to life, something in us comes to life. The lovely tune of a songbird evokes a sweetness in our hearts. The tenderness of a mama with her young is undeniable. The caressing sound of the waves or the trickling of a stream lapses the soul into a state of divine calm. The pitter-patter of raindrops and the cleansing quality of a good storm washes clean our worried minds. The fascinating mystery of the stars and the antiquity of the moon summons forth an appreciation of the eternal. The warmth and light of the sun gives way to all that is life. Admiring the seemingly simple lives of wildlife brings us comfort and escape, as we wish our hectic lives were only so simple.

In nature, we find the raw manifestation of creation. When one admires the intricate beauty, the stunning engineering, and the mind-boggling complexity that is present in the natural world, the questions that come to mind are: How can all this be a mistake? How can all this come from nothing? Can a "big bang" bring about such perfection and order in the midst of such savagery? Where does the evolution of evolution begin? The first principle is this: Either *nothing* created everything and the processes by which it has evolved (which is scientifically impossible), or *something* did, and that something is God.

As a Catholic Christian, I believe that the God who brought about all created things was made manifest and was revealed perfectly in the person of Jesus Christ. As a Catholic, my faith is Trinitarian: I believe that God the Father, God the Son, and God the Holy Spirit are one in the same. I experience Jesus in a very personal manner. I pray to him, am reminded of him by various images, and I find it very easy to enter into a relationship with him. I experience the Holy Spirit by means of inspirations that come from one thing or another. The Holy Spirit comes in many different ways and often at times least expected, but he is the source of all that is of God. Those out-of-the-blue coincidences are often the Spirit's work. But my experience of God the Father is something quite different.

There are those who would like to cram the Holy Trinity into a simple box as "creator, redeemer, and sanctifier." The trouble with this line of thinking is that this theological box is one of purely function. Our God is not a functionary. One can't have a personal relationship with a function. God revealed himself in a specific way through a specific person: Jesus. Jesus referred to God as "Father," and one step further, "Abba," which basically means "Daddy." Their relationship was intimately personal. Our relationship with God is also to be intimately personal.

So how do we specifically experience God the Father, our creator and the creator of all that ever was and will be? How do we experience God, the Father of Jesus in whom we have our salvation and who is our Father, too? We do so in lots of ways, but most obviously and potently in the raw manifestation of his creation. But, it is so vitally, extremely important that our attention and focus do not stop there. Again, we do not worship creation. God is not simply a creator. All of creation directly points to the creator, and the creator desires a personal relationship with you and me, individually and as a people.

Everything we need to know for our salvation is found in Christ. Everything we need to know about living a good life here on earth is found in Christ. However, there are many valuable lessons that can be learned from created things and the natural world. And creation does indeed tell us something of the one who created it. We do have a need for nature. Nature does fill a void within us. It teaches us and reminds us of things we often forget or overlook. There is a healing quality in nature. There is a stillness and quiet present in nature that could cure our ADD-ridden world if we only seek it. Nature can teach patience to even the most fidgety, caffeine-sugar-high-speed-internet-techno-overdosed-money-crazed-pop-culture junkie.

We hear in the book of Genesis that God saw that his creation was good. Indeed it is good. But often that goodness is difficult for us to see. It remains hidden. What can God teach us about life by means of a bunch of trees and rocks? What is there to learn in looking at an ugly old catfish or a goofy bird? Can dealing with the elements or pursuing a fat fuzzy critter to eat for dinner be of any value? Sitting in a tree stand from sunup until sundown certainly isn't an activity for the sane, is it? What could possibly be holy and spiritually educating about such pursuits? We shall see!

CHAPTER 3

In the Beginning

MY LOVE OF THE OUTDOORS began literally before I can remember. Photographs and stories are all that I can base my earliest childhood outdoor experiences on. My dad likes to remind me of things such as me hooking into a big fish and being too excited and too scared to reel it in. The earliest memories that I can recall are of my brother and I fishing with dad out of our old aluminum boat, catching crappie and whatever else would bite on our minnows and jigs. I remember times when we'd pull out crappie after crappie for what seemed like hours on end. I can recall the excitement of hooking into the occasional bass and the exhilarating fight they'd dish out. I remember the thrilling anticipation of getting things packed up and making the preparations to go on those trips.

When we knew we were going fishing, my brother and I would go through our little tackle boxes (complete with engraved name plates) and imagine what kind of fish we might catch with the different lures we had. My mom would pack up food and extra clothes while dad would get the boat and all the more complicated things in order. When it came time to load up the van (the "Golden Eagle," as we called it), my mom would hand stuff off to my brother and me and we'd run it out to our dad, who had a specific place for everything. It was almost like a military drill — organized, quick, and efficient. When all was good to go, we'd jump into the Golden Eagle, say a prayer for safe travel, and head off to the lake.

Those rides seemed to take forever. I simply could not wait to get to the lake and start fishing. My anxiousness burned as hot as the vinyl seats in that big ol' non-air-conditioned van as we rolled down those scorching summer highways en route to our destination. I would try to keep myself occupied by looking at the latest Bass Pro Shops or Cabela's catalogs that I reverently thumbed through on an almost daily basis. Of course, if things got too antsy, my brother and I would find some ridiculous way to keep ourselves entertained, which usually aggravated our parents to the point of them having to take disciplinary action with us.

The thing that would always send me over the edge is when we had to stop to get gas. My dad had a unique ritual of checking out the mechanical well-being of the van and meticulously cleaning every window while the gas tank was filling up. It used to drive me crazy! Didn't he know that we were supposed to drive as fast as possible without stopping for anything, no matter what, so we could get to the lake as fast as possible . . . so we could start fishing as fast as possible . . . so we could start having a great time as fast as possible!? And if the gas station ordeal didn't test my poor infantile patience enough, the bait shop most certainly would. Now, I loved going to the bait shop. I loved to check out all the neat lures, tackle, and fascinating fishing paraphernalia. But again, I liked to do it as fast as possible so I could get to fishing. My dad enjoyed going to the bait shop as well, but more than anything else he liked talking to the bait shop guys. And boy could he talk! I would race up and down the aisles in a panicked frenzy as my dad would casually lean on the counter and talk about all sorts of things for what seemed like an eternity. I tried to look as impatient and hurried as possible to get my dad moving, but the conversation would seem to go on and on. And just when I thought they were finishing up, the bait shop guy would light up one more cigarette and yet another round of manly bait shop talk would ensue. It didn't dawn on me until later that these were all honored ceremonial rituals of the fishing culture. I didn't realize that one day I, too, would stop at gas stations to check things out, purchase last minute items, have to use the restroom because I drank a gallon of coffee, and take a break to stretch. I never thought that I, too, would one day actually enjoy chatting with the guys in the bait shop and swapping stories of testosterone-fueled endeavors. But sure enough, now I do.

I can say without any reservation that fishing was the love of my life as a young boy. I thought about it constantly. I dreamed of what adventures might possibly come to pass in the future. I read (actually, mostly looked at the pictures) stacks of fishing magazines and books. I watched Saturday morning fishing shows with an almost religious zeal. I reorganized my tackle box every week and practiced casting my rods as often as I could. Every once in a while I'd sneak into the basement and take out my dad's enormous tackle box, slowly open it up, and gaze in complete awe at the hundreds of lures he had in there. Being in the presence of that tackle box made me feel like Moses standing before the burning bush. To behold the contents of that majestic tabernacle of tackle filled me with an overwhelming sense of awe and respect.

Growing up, I spent as much free time as possible hanging out on the nearby creeks or strolling the banks of the Missouri River, which was just a short bike ride away from where we lived at the time. I simply could not get enough of anything that had to do with fishing or the outdoors. Though I played soccer and baseball and all of the things kids seem to do, in all honesty I did it only to appease my parents, who were a bit concerned with my outdoor obsession, and to get free hotdogs and soda after the

game! All I wanted to do was hang out in the woods and fish —
for anything — anywhere and anytime I could. Even at a very
young age, I was enraptured by the mystical quality that I found
in fishing. Here was an activity that allowed me to venture into
exciting new places, learn new things and reach in and connect
to a world that I could not see beyond the surface of the water.
Fishing was just as exciting to me as opening presents on Christmas morning. In fact, it still is! Who knows what one might
catch! Who knows what might happen before the day is done!
Who knows what lies in wait beyond the bank! The possibilities
of what could happen when I went fishing filled me with an
undying exhilaration. The adventure of seeing what was around
the next creek bend or learning my way around a new area never
became dull. The anticipation of when and what would take my
bait or hit my lure turned me into a bona fide fishing fanatic!

Even on short day trips to places that happen to have a lake,
pond, or creek nearby, I would grab my ever-growing tackle box,
my rod and reel, and venture off to what looked like a good spot
to fish. Sometimes my little arms would go numb from carrying
all my fishing stuff on those long walks around the lake. And
there I would sit, totally glued to the bank in a Zen-like trance for
the entire time. I didn't want to eat, sleep, go to the bathroom,
play games, or do anything that would take me away from the
water for even the slightest moment. I would totally immerse
myself into my surroundings and in what I was doing. My parents
would have to almost forcibly get me to leave when it was time to
eat supper or go home.

Even at that very young age, I was addictively drawn to those
places of relative solitude. Being outside, walking through the
woods, and admiring the festival of life that was all around me as
I fished affected me in a way I couldn't explain. It filled my boyhood heart with an uncontainable joy. It made me feel so alive.

Those moments spent fishing either with my family, friends, or by myself nurtured my soul and awakened within me an unstoppable, unquenchable thirst to get to know the one who was responsible for creating all the wonders of nature that I was experiencing.

That desire to really get to know God is what gave birth to a simple, yet deep, spirituality. I began to pray all the time. The prayer that I engaged in was nothing more than simply recognizing God's presence, thanking him for all the blessings and wonders that he had bestowed upon me, and talking to him. I would talk to God for hours on end at times. The more time I spent in the outdoors, the more I recognized God's handiwork all around me and the closer I grew to him. God became not only my God, but also my best friend. When I went fishing (or did anything else), I did it with God. I became fully and absolutely aware of God's presence at all times and in all things. I felt, and still do feel, as if God is right at my side twenty-four hours a day, seven days a week. There was, and still is, no greater joy than to do something I really love with God. God is still my best fishing buddy. God is still my best, not to mention most reliable, hunting partner. I always approached God in the same manner that a small child would approach a parent: with love, dependence, true friendship, and respect.

Unfortunately, there are many who have great difficulty in their relationship with God because of this parent-like quality. Many of our conceptions about what God is like are based on information and experiences of our own parents. If someone has very domineering and rather unpleasant parents, that influence usually carries over to that person's idea of God. For a person whose parents may have been unloving or even abusive, that person will often despise God, thinking that God also hates them and is out to do them harm. As stated earlier, we see in Scripture that Jesus referred to God as "Abba," which basically means "Daddy."

The God that Jesus revealed is a loving father who desires to have an intimate loving relationship with us, his children.

This, of course, does not mean that God is the kind of father or parent who is a spineless pushover. We also learn in Scripture that God wants us to be disciplined, responsible, just, merciful, hardworking, and willing to sometimes suffer for his sake. God the Father calls us to imitate the love of Jesus Christ, his son. The love of Christ is a love that willingly makes sacrifices for the good of the other. It is a love that puts aside all selfish desires for the benefit of someone else. The love of Christ is a love so strong that one would lay down his or her very life for the other; just as Christ willingly suffered and died for our sake.

So much of what we think about love has been manufactured by our consumer-driven culture. We're given all sorts of images of things that are supposed to represent love. We have warm, fuzzy teddy bears with boxes of chocolates, Cupid shooting his arrow of love, red roses, all sorts of heart-shaped doodads, and so on and so forth. These things are all fine and dandy, but real love, the self-sacrificing love of Christ that we are called to imitate, is most often a "tough love."

Tough love requires hard work and discipline, and it brings some very different images to mind. Tough love comes in the form of headaches and empty wallets. It's getting up at all hours of the night to take care of a crying baby. It's taking care of an aging parent. It's sacrificing valuable free time in order to lend a helping hand when you really don't want to. This kind of love isn't always pleasant, and it certainly doesn't make us feel good. In fact, it can seem like a crucifixion at times. But there is no greater love than this. There is no love as life-giving and fruitful as this. Because after the struggles and pain of the crucifixion, there is the joy of the resurrection, and this is a joy that lasts into eternity.

Of course, I didn't realize all that during my young, adventuresome days. These were lessons I'd learn as time went on. The most important thing those childhood experiences of God taught me was to keep my relationship with God childlike (not childish). Jesus reminds us in the gospels to approach God in this childlike manner. And, again, this means to humbly recognize our dependence on God — to trust him, to respect him, and most importantly to love him.

When we think that we alone are in control and that we don't have to be dependent on anyone for anything, we'll no doubt have a loud and painful wakeup call sooner or later. When we don't trust anyone but ourselves, we can end up hating ourselves. We come to realize that we betray ourselves more than anyone else. When we love no one but ourselves, we eventually realize that our "love" of self is nothing more than prideful vanity. It's our dependence, trust, respect, and love of God that allows us to be dependent, trusting, respectful, and loving of others. And when we learn to do that (as God desires), the kingdom of heaven is truly upon us.

CHAPTER 4

River Rats

AT THE TIME OF MY CHILDHOOD and early adolescence, my hometown of St. Charles, Missouri, was still relatively small but rapidly growing. St. Charles is a town rich in historical significance. It was founded in 1769 by Louis Blanchette, and is one of the oldest and most historic towns in Missouri. Located along the Missouri River and near the Mississippi River, St. Charles became a launching pad for early explorers, traders, and immigrants who were traveling west. St. Charles rapidly became a thriving riverfront trading town. Among other noteworthy details, St. Charles is where the Lewis and Clark rendezvous occurred. It's also where Missouri's first state capitol was built. To top that off, St. Charles was the familiar stomping grounds of the likes of St. Philippine Duchesne and Daniel Boone.

The adventuresome spirit of those early pioneers seemed to still dwell there when I was a boy. At the time, I lived just a short distance from the original historic riverfront area of St. Charles. In fact, that area would become my beloved stomping grounds as well. Any chance I could get, I would walk or ride my bike down to "Main Street," as it was called, and spend hours just wandering up and down those old cobblestone roads. I loved to check out the shops and interesting places of business that dwelled in the old brick houses, which still bore the scars of the days of horse and wagon. More than anything else, I was drawn to the river. If the water was down, I'd go out on the rock dikes and wing dams and spend hours skipping stones, whittling on driftwood, fishing, and sometimes just talking to God and thinking. That old Main Street area still holds a special place in my heart. When I can, which is rare these days, I sneak down there and spend time retracing the steps of my boyhood. I go back to that same rock dike, sit down on the same rock, think about the good old days, and look at how everything else has changed. Most of the once family-friendly stores and shops are now bars and nightclubs. What used to be one of my favorite riverbank hideouts and fishing spots is now a gambling boat complex. Where there used to be miles of rich farmland, there are now shoulder-to-shoulder condos, apartment complexes, and shopping centers. If one visits St. Charles today, it is quite obvious that it's come a long, long way from being a relatively small town. Today, it's a thriving metropolis and continues to grow at a breakneck speed.

It was in the third grade that I met my good buddy Jason, who would become one of my best friends to this day and a true brother, with whom I share a deep love of the outdoors. Though I met Jay in the third grade, we didn't become really good friends until the fourth. While I lived in the suburbs of St. Charles, Jay lived in the nearby, yet rural area of Orchard Farm, which seemed to me like a world apart. Jay did all the things that I was so intensely interested in. He and his dad would river fish, hunt, set limb lines, make their own stink bait, and do all sorts of fascinating outdoor stuff. Jay was interested in anything that had to do with hunting and fishing. It was that common bond that originally sparked our friendship. We'd sit in class and talk about huge catfish, draw gun logos on our notebooks, and swap fish stories and tackle tips. Sometimes Jay would come to school with shotgun shells still in his coat pocket, not to take vengeance on his classmates in a psychotic bloodthirsty fit of violence, like today's troubled youths that we hear about in the news, but simply because he was out hunting over the weekend and forgot to empty his pockets. It wasn't long before Jay and I began spending a lot of time hanging out and eventually fishing and hunting together.

While I learned a great deal about the outdoors from my dad, and he is the one who originally planted the seed that would blossom into a lifelong love affair with the woods and waters, Jay's dad, Don, was also a huge influence on me. My dad taught me lots in regards to fishing on lakes and ponds for bass, bluegill, crappie, and other game fish. He taught me to fly fish and tie my own flies at a very young age. He taught me about different kinds of wildlife and all sorts of things that I cherish, practice, and reflect on to this day. But it was Jay and Don who opened up a whole new world to me.

Don taught me the ways of the river. I learned about river fishing, by both traditional and commercial methods. Don took me along with Jay to set and check limb lines, trotlines, and other such fish trapping devices. The excitement of what might possibly be on that line or in that net was exhilarating! I couldn't get enough of it! It was Don who taught me about catching one's own bait and about perseverance in harsh conditions. There were times that I would sleep over at Jay's house and Don would wake us up at 4:00 A.M. to go on some sort of a mysterious mission. These missions usually involved going off to some undisclosed location to fish, catch crawdads (while still in my best Sunday clothes), check traps, build a fire, or collect hickory nuts. These missions were carried out come rain, snow, hail, or under any other unpleasant circumstance (within reason).

It was by means of those outdoor skill-building missions that I learned the reality that the show can and must go on. It was a revelation to understand that, yes, one can go fishing when most folks would stay home and do quite well. I learned that no matter what the natural world could dish out, opportunities still abound and can also be thoroughly enjoyed. Today, I still love fishing in the rain, snow, and sleet, because of those little missions.

All throughout grade school, high school, and still today as often as we can, Jay and I get together to fish, hunt, reminisce, and revisit those old farmland and river-bottom haunts. There is one place in particular that was always and still remains our official congregating spot: "The Club." The Club is a piece of property on the Mississippi River that belongs to Jay's family. Years ago, when Don was a young man, there was an actual clubhouse on the property, which was know as the "Bachelors Club." Though the clubhouse has been long gone for decades, the name stayed.

Over the years The Club has witnessed our coming of age. We'd meet there as kids to fish and talk about the great adventures we'd embark on when we got older. When we got older, in high school, we'd go back there with some of our friends, mostly to sneak cigarettes and beer, listen to music, talk about girls, discuss teenage troubles, and, of course, to fish. Today we go back there to remember our more youthful days, discuss manhood troubles, drink beer legally, talk about past and future adventures, and, you guessed it, fish. If that piece of land along that ol' muddy river could talk, boy could it tell some stories (many of which are not so fitting to recount nowadays, being that I'm a man of the cloth and all!).

There is one adventure in particular that Jay, Don, and I set out on that has remained of legendary status to this day (it also continues to bring about the scorn and displeasure of our mothers!). When Jay and I were freshmen in high school, we decided to spend our spring break camping out on an island in the Mississippi. This was a spot we'd gone to and fished many times prior and we thought it would be great to spend the better part of a week there. For months we made lists of supplies we would need. We meticulously planned out almost every minute of each day we would spend on that trip. We were worked up into an excited fever pitch! Finally, it was mid-March and spring break was upon us! Now March in Missouri is a strange month. One day it's a sunny 80 degrees, the next it's cold and rainy, and before it's all over, a winter storm may even be resurrected and blow through from somewhere. And despite what the weatherman predicted, that's exactly what happened on that trip.

That first day, as we packed our gear into the johnboat, we were already exhausted from insomnia due to our rabid excitement. When we were all ready to go, Don manned the old Evinrude motor, and after what seemed like an eternity trying to get it to turn over and start, we were off! Don gave us the customary warning to look out for wild Indians, river-dwelling villains, and the crazed Amazon women who were all possibly on our tail and planning our demise while we slowly sputtered up the river.

After we finally got to our destination, it took some time to pack up and move all our gear from the boat to the camping spot, which was in the middle of the island next to a back-water slough that ran through it. After getting everything set up for the most part, it was time to start enjoying the first day of that long-awaited trip. It was a sunny, beautiful, early spring day. The birds were singing and new growth was emerging all around us. Various flowers were desperately trying to bud forth and expose their hidden loveliness. The fish were biting, and all seemed to be right with the world. While Jay and I were enjoying the day's fun, Don had hunkered down in our little tent for an afternoon nap.

As afternoon turned into evening, we found ourselves lounging around a crackling campfire discussing the finer points of fishing for carp and bullhead. As night began to fall, I made my way into the tent with the still fast asleep Don (those early risers just can't keep up!). Jay decided to sleep out under the stars next to the dwindling but still warm fire. As we prepared for slumber we noticed that Don had all of our sleeping bags. He was laying on one, was in another, and had the third on top of him. I wrestled mine off of the old rascal and Jay decided he'd be warm enough by the fire. After trying to get somewhat comfortable, we closed our eyes and were fast asleep.

That peaceful and much-needed sleep quickly came to an end when an hour later I heard Jay holler something like, "Good God, it's coming our way!" What was coming our way was an ominous dark cloud that quickly blackened the starlit sky. Accompanying this cloudy blanket of death was a bone-chilling wind that seemed like it would sweep all in its path into oblivion. Without hesitation, Jay crammed himself into the small worn-out tent that was barely big enough for Don and I. Then it started. The rain began to fall and the wind began to howl like a crazed, ravenous wolf about to suck the lifeblood out of its ripped-apart prey.

Don, still asleep, began to roll over and squish me into the side of the tent as Jay desperately forced himself in tighter. To say that we were like sardines crammed together in a little tin can is putting it very lightly. As the rain picked up force, we all became painfully aware of just how old and shabby that tent was. Suddenly we found ourselves being hosed down by the frigid juice that ran through Mother Nature's veins. The shockingly cold rain powered through the countless tent holes of various sizes and unleashed a watery hell upon all three of us. Minutes went by like hours. As we lay there in freezing misery, we wondered how much worse it could get. It got worse. Much worse.

After we and all of our extra clothes and gear were soaked with chilling spring rain, the sound of the water hitting the tattered tent suddenly became a bit crisper — the rain had turned into sleet. Now our water-soaked selves and gear slowly but surely got a nice coating of ice to top things off. Just when we thought it couldn't get any worse, the sleet turned to snow. Several inches later, and after what seemed like a night spent in eternal damnation, we crawled out of our abused and ruined tent into a winter wonder/hell land.

Our hearts sank with the realization that all of our gear was both frozen and now hidden somewhere beneath the virgin snow. We were still in our warm-happy-sunny-day clothes and none of us brought any cold-weather gear. Our fire pit and collected wood had to be dug out like the unearthing of a frozen Neanderthal. As we all bleakly emerged around the frosty remains of our only source of heat, we luckily found we had plenty of charcoal lighter fluid and quickly scrambled to get a fire going. After we warmed up and realized we had to abandon most of our gear (which we never got back) we took to the task of trying to get home.

We stomped through the frozen tundra back to the boat. Upon our arrival, we discovered that the motor absolutely would not start. We also realized that we'd lost our one and only oar somewhere along the line. Of course, those were the days before cell phones and other life-saving gadgetry, so we had to fend for ourselves. The dozens of boats that were on the water the day before, enjoying that first taste of warm weather, were nowhere to be found. The river patrol was nowhere to be found. No one was to be found. We dug around in the ice and snow-covered driftwood and found a few old rotten two-by-fours, which became our paddles. With quickly freezing hands we piled in the boat, shoved off and headed for the other side. With the wind still howling like a wildcat that's just broken the spine of a little bunny, the rough waters of the Mississippi spewed cold water over the side of the out-of-control johnboat, and onto us with great gusto.

Within minutes, my soaked jeans became as stiff as a suit of armor as they froze solid. My feet had long gone numb. My face felt as if it were being sandblasted as the stinging wind hit me like the swift hand of mama slapping a foul-mouthed back-sasser. My hands hurt so bad that I can still feel the pain now just thinking about it. The mighty Mississippi sent us careening down the turbulent muddy waters until we finally crashed into shore several miles down the line. When we hit dry land, Don gave me a troubled look and began upchucking the vintage can of Vienna Sausages that he ate for breakfast.

As we crawled out of the busted up boat, our clothes cracked and popped as the ice broke free from the fabric. Only Don had any relative idea where we were. Stunned speechless from our endeavor, we followed Don through several farm fields as we headed somewhere. After a long trek on foot, we reached an old house and went to the door. After a quick conversation between Don and whoever lived there, we were rushed inside to get warm. Not too long after, Jay's sister came and picked us up.

When we finally made it back to Jay's house, we all just sat there, still half frozen, exhausted beyond belief and still speechless, except for the occasional four-letter word that eased out as an expression of relief. It seemed like it took weeks to finally thaw out completely. I caught hell from my parents for months after for being so ill-prepared. To this day, those who remember that fabulous outing still tease us. Whenever a good snowstorm kicks in, people tell us, "Hey, you guys better get over to the island! You don't want to miss out on this fine weather!" As it turns out, that wouldn't be the first time Jay and I would put our lives in serious jeopardy, all for the love of the outdoors. But that's another story.

After that fateful trip was over and my brain thawed out enough to think, I found myself getting very angry with God. I'd say to him, "What the heck was that all about? Here I prayed and trusted in you that this was going to be a great trip and that we were going to really have fun, and it turned out to be a nightmare! We could have gotten killed! Why did you do that to us?" It was the first time that I experienced not only my prayers not being answered, but it seems God did just the opposite of what I was praying for. It was the first time I learned that God's will is not my will. It was the first time I really learned about suffering and about carrying a cross.

You know, on any given day of the week, one can read the paper or watch the news, and quite easily be overcome by grief. On a daily basis we hear of terrible things both locally and worldwide. We hear of treacherous acts of violence, war, death, destruction, and ungodly injustices. We hear of the horrible things people do to one another and the atrocities that many innocent people are forced to suffer day after day. To top that off, there are those personal struggles that we deal with — financial difficulties, problems with our health, addictions, the loss of a loved one, being out of work, troubled relationships, a vacation gone terribly wrong. The list goes on and on.

In the wake of these things, it can be easy for us to find ourselves in despair. Sometimes it seems like the whole world is crumbling around us. How often we cry out to the Lord for guidance, for peace, for healing, and for hope — and yet, at times, it seems like our prayers are in vain. Sometimes it's difficult to find that ray of light as we journey through those dark and weary days.

There is a passage in the Gospel of Luke where we hear Jesus giving the disciples the great reality check. He tells them about what's soon to happen to him. While Jesus brought healing, peace, hope, and the love of God to everyone he encountered, everywhere he went, he reminds the disciples that he, the Son of God, will experience suffering just like the rest of us. He, the Son of God, will experience betrayal, humiliation, and rejection just like the rest of us. He, the Son of God, will die just as we all will one day die. But, he, the Son of God, will rise from the dead, and by means of his resurrection, we, too, are given the hope of resurrection and eternal life.

We obviously live in a wonderful world, in a world filled with incredible beauty. But nonetheless, our world is unfortunately dominated by sin. That first sin of Adam and Eve, that "original sin" of rejecting God, has poisoned everyone and everything in our world from then until now. Death, disease, personal tragedy, horrific acts of violence, and injustices are not punishments for sin, but they certainly can be the result of sin. AIDS is not a punishment for deviant sexual behavior and drug use, but it can be a result. Lung cancer and heart disease is not a punishment for abusive smoking, but it can be a result. Homelessness, hunger, poverty, war, all the things that plague our world all have their roots somewhere, at some point in time, in sin, in that initial turning away from God. And, unfortunately, *all* of mankind suffers as a result of the sins of mankind.

Sin has a tremendous domino effect. One person's sin can cause a chain reaction that can negatively affect the lives of many innocent people and sometimes that effect doesn't show up and manifest itself until many years down the road. We all love the ability to freely choose our own path, to freely make decisions for ourselves; we all love the free will that God has given us, but the flip side is that our choices and decisions can give birth to tremendous destruction — personal destruction, social destruction, and spiritual destruction.

With all that being said, though, we still see innocent children dying from Leukemia. We see perfectly healthy people suddenly being struck down with a terrible disease. We even saw a Pope (John Paul II) suffer the crippling effects of Parkinson's disease. We see so many bad things happening to so many good people. What we often don't see, or don't realize, however, is that just as many bad things happen to bad people. The reality is that bad things happen to *all* people. The bottom line is that we live in an imperfect world. As an old philosophy instructor once pointed out, our world can produce someone as good and holy as Mother Teresa or someone as evil as Adolf Hitler. Our world can produce something as beautiful as a rainbow or something as destructive as a tornado. The bad things in our world are something we all experience. Some experience it to a greater degree, some to a lesser degree. For some it is a direct result of their own sinfulness, poor choices, or bad decisions; for others, it's the result of someone else's sinfulness, poor choices, or bad decisions. And many of these poor choices and bad decisions are not originally made with ill intent. Who would have known thirty years ago that exposure to certain things would cause cancer? Who would have known that certain things in our diet and our environment that we took for granted could eventually do us much harm? Who would have known that building houses and subdivisions in a particular place (or camping out on a particular island) would one day be in the direct path of a natural disaster?

Many theologians over the years have stated that Jesus did not come to remove suffering from the world. He instead came to enter into our suffering with us. It is he who wishes to comfort us in our suffering. It is he who teaches us to take up our cross and to follow him. And as much as we'd like to, we can't pick and choose our crosses. For some, the cross might be a terrible physical illness; for others, a mental illness. Some might experience the cross by means of an addiction or a struggle with a particular sin. The cross may come in the form of nonstop relationship problems. It may be the constant search for more meaningful employment. It may be a disastrous spring break. All of us have a cross to carry.

Sometimes we like to think that our particular cross is heavier than someone else's. We say, "Yeah, that person has to work a lousy demeaning job to support their family, but look at what I have to go through with this or that! Yeah, that person doesn't get along with their parents/spouse/whoever, but look at this terrible illness I have!" No matter what our particular cross may be, it all boils down to the same thing for each of us: suffering.

The Son of God also teaches us that our suffering can at times be beneficial. Sometimes it's only by means of suffering that we finally open our eyes to things we have been ignoring. Sometimes our suffering can teach us a much-needed, life-changing lesson. Our suffering can be offered up to God as a powerful form of prayer as we unite our suffering to those of Jesus on the cross.

Ultimately, it is Jesus who teaches us how to carry our cross. He challenges us to take up our cross daily and to follow him. Some days that cross is heavier than other days. Some days our cross is different from the previous days. But, when we pick up that cross, we, too, get a reality check. We realize that, indeed, no one is exempt from suffering. We realize that we do live in an imperfect world that can dish out some pretty miserable stuff from time to time. We realize that as our bodies and minds are beaten down with pain and illness, and as our emotions are put through a meat grinder, our souls can grow stronger if we unite that suffering and offer that suffering to Christ.

We realize that surrendering our suffering to God can bring us peace in the midst of strife, joy in the midst of sadness, hope in the midst of fear, and love in the midst of hate. We realize by means of our crosses that we are not made to last in this world. We are made for eternity. We are made to be God's children. And carrying our crosses with dignity, with faith, and as a prayerful sacrifice, even though we may seem to be losing our lives in the process, is what leads us to our eternal life and our heavenly home.

CHAPTER 5

Trout Fishing Revelation

By THE TIME I WAS in high school I already had quite a few notches on my fishing rod. I had honed my skills a great deal and continued to seek out new places, techniques, and information regarding the pursuit of fishing. Although I had half-heartedly fished for trout on a few occasions over the years, it didn't interest me all that much at the time. When I thought of trout fishing, what came to mind were visions of tiny little fish caught on itsy bitsy flies, which were cast on long, flimsy rods. I associated trout fishing with extremely wealthy, well-to-do, high-falooting business people who had way too much money and who took those little fish way too seriously. I pictured yuppies driving up in their luxury cars, assembling their thousand dollar fly rods, approaching the river decked out in the latest fly-fishing fashions that they purchased at some elite outdoor apparel boutique. (Let me make it very clear that I'm not bad-mouthing any particular social class here. This was simply the stereotypical impression I had at the time.)

The other image I associated with trout fishing was the opposite extreme; shoulder-to-shoulder with hundreds of half-drunk hooligans, throwing cigarette butts in the water, fishing with night crawlers and yelling at the jerk who just cast over their line once again. Needless to say, when a buddy invited me to go trout fishing,

I was more than a bit hesitant. But, after a little further consideration, I decided to give it a shot. I really had no idea what I was getting into, but it was rather exciting getting geared up for this relatively new adventure I was about to embark on. After some quality time spent at the local sporting goods store, I had everything I needed to get started in this trout-fishing stuff. I had my clumsy rubber chest waders, my multi-pocketed tan fishing vest, a light spinning rod and reel, and all the other little gadgets that I would need while on the water.

Finally the day came and we hit the highway in the direction of Lake Taneycomo (located in southwest Missouri) for my first serious trout-fishing adventure. That first morning of the trip we woke up at 4:30 A.M., grabbed a quick bite to eat, piled into truck, and drove a short distance to the water. Though Lake Taneycomo is called a "lake," it's actually more like a fast-flowing river, or slow-rolling stream, depending on how much water is coming through Table Rock Dam, which is where Taneycomo begins. As advised, I put on several layers of clothing underneath my waders to insulate me from the extremely cold water that flowed from the bottom of Table Rock Lake into the headwaters of Taneycomo.

After we suited up and got our rods rigged, we headed down to the water with flashlights in hand. In the damp black morning, our feeble electric lights were not much good, being that the fog was so thick we couldn't see more than a few yards in front of us. And even though it was summer, it didn't take long for me to start to shiver in the frigid waist-deep water. There was a curious smell of fish in the pungent morning mist, and as we descended into what seemed like a great black hole I found myself slipping and sliding on the slick moss-covered rocks. I heard the guttural squawk of a great blue heron nearby and the distant honking of geese as I blindly stumbled along, trying to follow my buddies through this ebony chasm.

Suddenly, the light in front of me stopped moving and I heard a whisper, "This is the spot." We stopped — where, I had no idea — and cast our night crawlers into the black nothingness. I heard a little "plop" and felt my line tighten up in the slow moving water as my rig settled on the bottom. There I stood, still more than half asleep, already freezing to death, in total darkness, fishing with a big fat night crawler impaled on a little bitty hook. "So this is trout fishing," I thought to myself. I had to admit that the whole ordeal of just getting to that spot was incredibly exciting! It was like some secret covert Special Forces operation. But now what? Would I have to stand there for hours on end before a fish would bite? Not long after I asked myself that question, which was only a few minutes after getting into position, I felt a sudden erratic tugging on my line. With the final tug, I knew there was a fish on. I set the hook and, after a thrilling battle, landed my first serious trout. Still fishing completely blind, we each landed several good fish with the aid of our quickly dimming flashlights.

A couple of hours later something happened that I would never forget: the sun came up! Now I've obviously seen the sun come up many a times before and it's always a beautiful, magical sight, but watching the sun come up on Lake Taneycomo while trout fishing was one of the most transforming experiences of my life! The pitch black evolved into a dark blue, then a medium gray, and finally radiant beams of sunlight pierced the morning sky, illuminating the fog with a radiating white light! I still could not see the bank, or anything else in the immediate distance, but the vibrant sun-lit fog that surrounded us was absolutely breathtaking. The black hole of the pre-dawn morning had transformed into a golden, heavenly, glowing utopia! I thoroughly expected to see St. Peter at some point. I felt as if I was standing before the very gates of heaven!

As the morning continued on, catching fish was really of no concern to me. I was completely caught up in what seemed like the dawning of a new creation. It was a true revelation of the glory of God! As the fog lifted and morning turned into afternoon, I slowly began to focus more on the actual fishing. While I continued to learn the ropes in the ways of catching trout, I quickly noticed that indeed my preconceived notions were true! I did see lots of tiny little fish being caught on itsy bitsy flies, cast with long flimsy rods. I did see wealthy, well-to-do, high-falooting business people with way too much money taking these little fish way too seriously. I did see yuppies driving up in their luxury cars, assembling their thousand dollar fly rods, approaching the river decked out in the latest fly fishing fashions that they no doubt purchased at some elite outdoor apparel boutique.

Sure enough, I also saw people fishing shoulder-to-shoulder and half-drunk hooligans swigging flasks of whiskey and throwing cigarette butts in the water. Wouldn't you know it; I saw people fishing with night crawlers (including myself) and people yelling at the jerk next to them who just cast over their line once again. Basically, I saw people of all walks of life, of all different social classes, of various races, places, genders, and all ages doing the same thing in lots of different ways. They all were there to experience the captivating beauty that I had witnessed for the first time that day. They all were there to enjoy the scrappy fight those fish put out. They all were there to witness God's handiwork and admire the hand-painted beauty of those marvelous fish. Though everybody was expressing it and searching for it in different ways, I think everybody there was fishing for something much more satisfying than a pretty little fish, and I believe everybody enjoyed a good catch that day!

That trip was all it took for me to get helplessly hooked on trout fishing. The trout bug had indeed bitten me hard and injected me with a terribly infectious, lethal, dose of troutfishing fever! When I got home from that trip I began reading everything I could get my hands on regarding trout fishing. I quickly upgraded my trout gear and traded in my night crawlers for something a bit more challenging, productive, and exciting. I watched dozens of trout-fishing videos, tied hundreds of different flies, and assembled my own spinners and small crank baits. I researched trout waters that were in the area, and practiced my fly-fishing techniques with renewed enthusiasm. I studied fish biology and learned all I could about ecology as it applied to trout and their habitat. I was on an all-out quest, boldly exploring a fascinating new world of fishing that had opened up before me.

The newfound freedom of wade fishing empowered me to get off the bank, get into the water, and actively stalk my prey. I was no longer landlocked or dependent on someone with a boat to expand my opportunities on the water. Trout fishing allowed me to do the things I loved about the outdoors all at once. It's sort of a combination of hiking, swimming, hunting, and fishing all in one.

I quickly found out that there were a good number of places that I could trout fish that were not much more than an hour away. I also discovered that there were tons of creeks and streams nearby that I could fish for small mouth bass and the like and basically get the same experience, just without the trout. I vigorously studied maps and started visiting and fishing every location there was in the area. Some were great, some were not so great.

After several months of exploring and checking out new bodies of water, I narrowed things down to just the really good places. These were places that not too many people knew about, or that a lot of folks would not bother fishing because of the physically demanding maneuvers it would take to actually access the water. These were also places where I would often be the only guy out there all day. It was rare to see someone else on the water, even though these were not "top secret" locations. I had about a half dozen streams, rivers, and creeks that I began to primarily focus my efforts on. Of those, I picked two of which over time I would come to intimately know like the back of my hand — "home waters," as they say.

It was on these home waters that I put to the test this wealth of knowledge that I had rather recently acquired. I tried out countless techniques and theories, constantly experimenting with different fly patterns and lures that I made. I was not concerned with exclusively becoming either a fly fisherman or a spin fisherman. I did both (and still do), because I enjoy them both. One is a nice change of pace from the other. It didn't take long for me to discover what worked and what didn't work. And, as I was rapidly gaining lots of on-the-job experience and catching a good number of fish, I soon began to focus my efforts on bigger fish. Ah yes, the time had indeed come that I wanted to go after trophy fish.

As I continued to ponder my newly acquired trout fishing knowledge and compared it to my experiences with other species of fish, I came to believe, without a doubt, that there are universal principles that apply to certain fish no matter where one is fishing. One of those principles is this: a large predator fish, whether it's a trout or bass or whatever, will not waste his or her precious, limited, life-sustaining energy fooling with tiny morsels of food *when at the same time* he or she is offered something big, meaty, and nourishing that is easy to catch. With that in mind I began to tie different flies that imitated good-sized bait fish. Along with that I used crank baits and spinners that also imitated indigenous baitfish. Whether I fished a fly, crank bait, or spinner, I focused on fishing it slowly, with a few twitches and pops here and there to make it look alive and in trouble. And by golly it worked!

Using this technique as the foundation for everything else I did, I started catching much bigger fish. Of course, one also has to know where to look for bigger fish, but sure enough, I found that a big ol' hungry trout (or anything else) simply could not resist what it thought was a fat, juicy minnow slowing moving along. If you've been working hard all day and are too worn out to cook a decent meal for yourself, are you going to turn down an opportunity from someone who wants to treat you to a delicious prime rib dinner? I don't think so! The same applies to fish.

As I began to dedicate my efforts more precisely toward catching trophy fish, I realized that some bodies of water are naturally going to be much more productive than others regarding producing and growing these bigger fish. The term "trophy" is relative to several factors. A trophy fish that is caught in one body of water may be considered average size in another. Generally speaking, though, I think most fishermen would consider a trout of 20 inches or more, or a trout that weighs five pounds or more, a trophy fish.

The location that I was most heavily fishing at the time did have some big fish in it. I saw pictures and heard stories of people catching four- and five-pounders and even a big nine-pounder in the not-so-distant past, but these catches were very rare. Even after several years of fishing one particular area known for trophy fish, the biggest I'd personally seen was a five-pound rainbow trout that a friend caught and a half-dead, six-pound brown trout that I found washed up on the bank one morning. I'd caught several large fish there over the years, but didn't actually catch a trophy rainbow (five pounds) from that body of water until recently.

Without much thought, I realized that my best chance of catching a serious trophy trout was to go back to where my love of trout fishing was initially spawned: Lake Taneycomo. It is no secret that Lake Taneycomo had been producing monster trout for years. Catching rainbow trout in the five-pound range and bigger was not all that rare. This was also the place to go for gigantic brown trout. After all, the Missouri brown trout record (at the time) of 23 pounds was caught there by local fishing legend Marty Babusa. Bigger ones have been caught since.

In preparation for my trophy trout hunt, I watched, over and over again, an instructional video that featured Mr. Babusa. I watched it so many times that I even memorized his lines. Marty Babusa quickly became my trout-fishing idol. You can imagine the thrill when on my next trip to Taneycomo I found myself on the water fishing downstream from Marty. He had the mystique and appearance of a mountain man. He had a big scruffy beard, dressed in camouflage, and was not afraid to use what would appear to be unconventional techniques in the scrutinizing eyes of some of the fly-fishing community. He moved slowly and, like a phantom, would simply appear and disappear at different points along the river. Here is a guy who consciously stalked particular fish and knew the value of applying certain principles relative to that fish in order to catch that particular fish. That is what I wanted to learn to do.

It was on that trip that I began to try out some of these different big-fish techniques and put my recently concocted flies and lures to the true test. It was late October, and being that my dad and I were there during the middle of the week, there were not very many other fishermen out on the water. This allowed me to really get down to business. On the second day of our trip, I spotted a giant trout hanging out behind a big rock. I'm not sure if it was a rainbow or brown, but it was huge, most likely in the neighborhood of eight to ten pounds. I started casting my fly with great caution, not to spook him. He didn't budge. He just lazily watched my fly drift by time and time again. I even grazed his mouth a few times and bounced it off his head with very little reaction other than him darting off only to return to the same spot moments later.

I must have tried every fly I had with the same results. As of that year, using live bait of any kind within the first five miles from the dam had become illegal. So even though I was tempted to go back to my roots and throw a big greasy worm in front of him or a chunky minnow of some kind, I couldn't. I fished for that trout for hours with no luck at all. I returned the next day, and, would you believe it, there was that fish in the same spot! I decided to try something different and broke out my trusty spinning rod and left the fly rod in the van. I cast every spinner I had in front of that fish and again he ignored them all. Usually one can eventually get a big fish to bite out of anger or aggravation if nothing else, but this guy was as calm as a cucumber. During one of those fruitless rounds, the warning horns sounded off, which meant we had to get to dry land quick or drown in the extremely fast rising water that was about to be generated through the dam. And so, day two came to an end, again producing no trophy fish.

For weeks before, and all during that trip, I was absolutely, totally, and completely consumed with thoughts of catching a trophy trout. I was obsessed! It's all I thought about. When on the water I would be in that Zen-like fishing trance of my childhood. Nothing could pull me away, except the threat of drowning, which is very much a reality when fishing next to a dam. Day three came and again that fish stayed true to its territorial instincts and was in almost the same spot. But that day things were different. He was hungry! He did not stay in one place for too long. He would swim around, hold up in a certain spot looking for food, then zoom off to a different spot. He was working in this circular pattern for some time.

That day I again opted for my spinning rod, complete with a good-sized minnow crank bait. I was not always sure where he was, so I, too, fished in a circular pattern that afternoon hoping to cut him off at the pass. Again, some time had passed with no action. Then out of the blue, I noticed someone moving in on my right. It was Marty Babusa! No doubt he knew that monster fish was there and he, too, was after it. I was nervous just being in the presence of such fishing greatness, even though we didn't even acknowledge each other's presence. I continued to methodically cast my lure, covering every foot of my immediate area, when all of a sudden my rod doubled over and almost flew out of my hand! The drag began to scream and line ripped off the reel fast and furiously. I knew I had him! My thoughts were confirmed when I saw in the crystal clear water an absolute whale of a trout on the other end of my line!

My God, I had him! Now what? Being that this was by far the biggest trout I could even imagine being able to hook into, my mind franticly raced with thoughts of what to do and what not do in order to land this beast. I knew I had to keep him out of the snags, not put too much pressure on him or try to horse him in. I had to just try and wear him down as best I could. My heart beat so fast and loud that I thought it might explode. Every beat felt like a stick of dynamite going off in my chest. I could feel it throughout my entire body. All my surroundings went still and quiet. I was in that zone where there is only you and your object of focus, and everything else melts away. It was as if everything was happening in slow motion. With every millisecond I prayed to God to help me land that fish. "Please don't let me lose him! Please don't let him get off my line! Oh God, please!"

Suddenly, in the midst of this epic battle, I noticed someone slowly approaching out of the corner of my eye. It was Marty. He must have seen my excited distress and he came over to coach me through the fight. He unhooked the net from the back of my vest and was prepared to help me land that massive fish. Out in the water I caught a few more glimpses of the titan as he rolled over and swam from side to side. His brightly colored girth appeared to be the size of a watermelon (well, maybe not quite that big)! Still, my rod verged on breaking. Still, my reel begged for mercy. Still, I pleaded with the Almighty to come to my aid.

And then it happened. Just as I thought victory was eminent, the tremendous pressure on my rod and reel was released as I heard a dissonant, "pinck!" He broke me off! My rod returned to its straight position. My line went limp and my heart sank to the bottom of the river and was washed down stream like a lifeless rotting catfish that's been sucked through the violent churning turbines of Table Rock Dam. He was gone. Marty, feeling my pain, gave me a knowing look and said, "Well, one thing's for sure, that's a fish you'll never forget." Boy was he right about that. The remainder of the trip, and for several weeks after, I sulked in a broken silence. I was utterly crushed. I had never felt the agony and bitterness of defeat so intensely in all my life.

That fish still remains embedded in my memory to this day. Every fisherman has an encounter with "the one that got away," and that was mine. Some may laugh and wonder what the big deal is. After all, it's just a fish, right? Wrong. It's not just about losing a fish. It's about the time and effort that seems to have all been in vain. It's about expended energy and disciplined intensity harnessed for one single-minded purpose and goal, which now lies dead. But it's also about the motivation to do better the next time around. It's also about the reality that all that homework did, in fact, pay off, to a point. It's the realization that we can achieve something quite significant if we put our minds to it and are willing to put in the hours. To sum it up, "Close," as they say, "but no cigar!" Oh, but we will meet again mighty Lake Taneycomo trophy trout . . . we will meet again!

CHAPTER 6

Fishing With a Vengeance

THE TRAUMATIC LOSS of what would have been my first and biggest trophy trout of all time haunted me like an angry ghost. Everywhere I looked I was reminded of that fateful day that had gone so terribly amok. The pictures of happy fisherman holding magnificent trout in those glossy photos that filled the fishing magazines seemed to mock me. Every time I saw a noble, well-aged, mounted trout hanging on a wall somewhere, I was certain I could hear it laughing at me and sneering a despised, lifeless grin, as though it knew its distant relative had valiantly defeated me in battle.

If I heard through the grapevine of someone else I knew catching a remarkable trophy fish, I became insanely jealous. That fish ruined me! My contempt for that Lake Taneycomo bruiser who humiliated me so badly burned like a heavy stinking pot of molten lead! I vowed that I would be redeemed! I was not going to simply scratch this one off the list as "the one that got away." This was a personal vendetta!

I began to ask more questions and dive further into the study of big fish. I visited several fly shops and outdoor stores in search of some sound advice from local experts. I quickly discovered that this was pretty much a futile effort. Many of these "experts" were very knowledgeable in the ways of entomology and could almost predict the exact time of various insect hatches. They also knew the finer points of employing all the high-tech gear that was on the market. I curiously and respectfully listened to their advice and where-with-all in regards to what they firmly believed were the keys to catching trophy fish. But every time I asked the million dollar question, "So what's the biggest trout you've caught?" most of these "experts" would begin to stutter and mumble and come up with a rather pathetic tale of catching some "huge" two-pound fish. Two pounds! I wanted to catch fish that would eat two-pounders for breakfast!

Disappointed with most of the feedback I got from local fishermen, I decided I had to go back to my initial "prime rib dinner" philosophy of fishing, inspired by Marty Babusa. I began to take to heart the words my of my dad, who always told me, "Most fishing lures and equipment are made to catch fishermen, not fish." I began to once again be disgusted with the whole trout-fishing scene. The insulting high prices and low quality of fly-fishing gear filled me with a sickened contempt. The elitist attitude of many fly fishermen I ran into aggravated the tar out of me, as did the opposite extreme of the undermining cheating tactics of slob fishermen.

Filled with rage (though a fun-filled rage), I went back to the drawing board and re-examined everything that I had come to know about trout fishing thus far. I went through all my fishing gear and got rid of all the gadgets and silly junk that I didn't need or that was not productive. I traded in my traditional fly-fishing vest for a crude chest/back pack that I fashioned myself from old military surplus items. I narrowed down my hundreds of flies to just the patterns that had proven themselves time and time again no matter where, when or what conditions I fished.

I stocked my one remaining fly box with a good supply of mostly just four patterns: the San Juan worm, a scud pattern, my "jigabugger," and my "deadly white jig." The San Jaun worm and scud patterns (along with some other weird stuff I tied up just for fun) I would only use if I got a wild hair to try something other than the jigabugger or deadly white jig. The jigabugger is basically a variation of the tried and true "wooly bugger." I tie this pattern on larger-sized black jig heads, but not too big that I can't cast it well with a five-weight fly rod. I use a lot of marabou on the tail to give it a thick appearance, wrap it with gold ribbing and trim down the hackle quite a bit just so the whole thing looks fuzzy. I tie it in shades of medium olive. (If you don't tie flies you'll have no idea what I'm talking about here, but that's okay.) I made these variations to give this fly sort of a fat and juicy appearance. I'm not sure if the fish think it's a crawdad, a chubby little baitfish, or some other of their favorite delights, but they like it! They love it! They can't get enough of it!

I developed my "deadly white jig" after reading many articles on the undeniable fish-catching power of micro jigs that imitate threadfin shad. As it turned out, these little white jigs were very potent on the White River system, especially during the cold months when thousands of dead shad would be sucked through the dams. The trout apparently would gobble up these tasty bits in an uncontrollable feeding frenzy.

As I researched more about these little white jigs, I kept thinking back to the fishing of my youth. Almost everything I had fished for over the years would pounce on a minnow when given the opportunity. I always thought to myself, "If I could only fish one lure for the rest of my life, what would it be?" The answer always came up the same: a little to medium-sized minnow crank bait. After all, that's what I caught (and lost) that devilish big trout on! In trying to simplify the matter even more, I asked myself, "Would a shad/minnow imitation only be incredibly effective during certain months? If these trout are so crazy about shad, minnows, and the like when the pickings are easy, why wouldn't they be even more crazy about them when the pickings are slim?" I realized that certain species of baitfish and other trout food are more abundant at certain times of the year, so I asked my self this question: "Do I only like to eat prime rib a few times a year? Wouldn't I whoof it down any chance I could possibly get if it were available?" The answer, of course, was a mouthwatering "yes!"

With that matter settled, I wanted to create a fly that had the same qualities of a deadly minnow crank bait and that would have a year-round appeal. I began to experiment with different fly patterns, and after many prototypes and lots of trial and error, I finally tied up a design that I liked. It had the flash, the meatiness, the action, and the appeal of a minnow, but could be fished with ease on a relatively light fly rod. Now it was time to put it to the test!

I began to fish the "deadly white jig" everywhere I went, in various conditions. I fished it on hot days, cold days, at night, in the morning, in the afternoon, in clear water, and in muddy water. I fished it on sunny days, on rainy days, and on overcast days as well. I fished it on every trout stream in the area. I fished it on wild trout, on hatchery trout, and on any combination of the two. I dead drifted it under a strike indicator, I stripped it in, and tried every other presentation I could think of. I tallied up the results and in all cases they were the same: success! Overwhelming success! I had never fished anything so successful in all my life! I knew I was on to something that would revolutionize (and greatly simplify) the way I fished.

At last the time came to put the "deadly white jig" to the ultimate test and return to the scene of my bitter defeat: Lake Taneycomo. It was a year later and I once again headed out for what was becoming an annual event: the Lake Taneycomo October fish-a-thon. On the first day of the trip my dad and I arrived in the early afternoon, unpacked, got things organized, and headed over to the lake to fish for the remainder of the evening. There were a number of people on the water that day, and as I waded over to one of my favorite spots I noticed that not too many folks were catching fish.

Things were in kind of a lull at the moment. I decided to position myself a good respectful distance from the other fisherman and thus begin casting the DWJ (deadly white jig) into the chilly, trout-infested waters of Taneycomo. I'll be darned if I didn't hook into a fish on the first cast! Within a half hour I had pulled out a dozen fish. I began to get troubled and curious looks from those around me as if perhaps I had some kind of cheat tactic going on. The fisherman on each side of me began to close in a bit to get a better look at what I was doing. Some even began to question me. I reassured them that I was not baiting, chumming, shuffling, snagging, or anything else. I was simply fishing the DWJ.

I want to point out that my intention here is not to toot my own horn or give the reader the impression that the DWJ is some magical fly that *makes* fish bite out of some kind of voodoo spell it emits. Sometimes it does not produce much at all, but on those days neither does anything else. Sometimes I'll only catch a few fish the whole day with it, but those are times when nothing else is catching fish at all. The simple fact is that if there are hungry or temperamental fish around, they will eat the DWJ.

The next day of the October fish-a-thon produced similar results; lots of trout were caught on the DWJ while other flies I tried didn't produce squat. As my confidence continued to build, I officially dubbed the DWJ endeavor a smashing success. But now it was time to focus my efforts on what I really came for: redemption! And so I moved off to deeper, darker waters where I knew the big boys liked to roam.

After some time, I made visual contact with a large rainbow trout. He was cruising up and down on the edge of a current break where shallow water met deep water. I could see he was hungry. With the cloud cover that afternoon it was hard to keep an eye on him, so I had to just continue working over the general area. Nothing happened for quite a while. Just when I was about to give up and move down stream, my strike indicator disappeared. I set the hook, thinking I was probably hung up on the bottom when all of a sudden a forceful explosion bent my rod like a wet noodle. My reel screamed as line began to rush upstream in the direction of the locomotive fish attached to the other end. My dad, who happened to be upstream, gave me an affirmative signal that indeed I was hooked up with a big one.

My heart began to pump so hard it was almost painful. My whole body shook as if I was having some kind of toxic withdrawal. My entire being was instantly taken back to that moment a year earlier (almost to the day) when my dreams of catching a trophy were crushed by that mean ol' hulk of a trout. I began to plead with God, "Please don't let me lose him! Please don't let him get off this time! Please help me land this fish! Please God, please!" That fish had stripped all the fly line off my reel and now I was down to the backing. I knew I had to start to turn things around and get the upper hand in this bout.

I slowly and evenly began to apply pressure to the fish. I would gain several yards of line, then he'd take out a few. This back and forth game of tug-of-war went on for several minutes, but I was slowly winning the battle. I finally got the fish in close enough and landed him with one fell-swoop of the net. Dad and I walked over to a nearby gravel bar to have a look and weigh, measure, and photograph the fish. It was a beauty! It was a perfect specimen of a rainbow trout: long, richly colored, heavy, yet symmetrical.

A lot of the really big fish in Taneycomo are trout that were used in the hatchery for brood stock. After they did their duty, they would be released into the lake. These brood stock fish are easily recognized by their gnarly appearance: worn-off fins from being in the concrete runways, ugly scars and discoloration. This fish, much to my elated pleasure, was not a released brood stock. He didn't have a mark on him, and all his fins were perfectly intact. This was a true river fish who'd either been naturally spawned or who had gown up and survived for many years after his initial release from the hatchery as a young'un.

My hands still trembled as I got out my scale and tape measure. This gorgeous fish weighed in at five pounds and was twenty-one inches in length. I was on cloud nine! This fish was not nearly as big as the hog I lost the previous year, but nonetheless, I felt redeemed. I had finally caught my first trophy trout.

After the initial satisfaction of catching that fish wore off, (which was several weeks) I found that instead of being at ease and content with this wonderful catch, I was instead now filled with a terrible desire to catch more and bigger trophies. I had officially become a "trophy hunter," which is something I never thought I would evolve into. For the next several years, the now biannual trip to Taneycomo, as well as any other place or opportunity to trout fish, became an all-out hunt for trophies. It became such an obsession that if no one else was able to join me on those trips, then I'd go myself. I was selfishly focused on one thing and one thing only: trophy trout. The camaraderie and companionship of family and friends began to take a back seat to my heartless fish-catching desires. Appreciating and even noticing the stunning, surreal beauty that first attracted me to this sport was replaced by a cold, though unstoppable will to catch every trophy trout that dwelled in every stream and every river in the entire state of Missouri! The once peaceful and prayerful journeys to and from those lovely locations had become a fast and furious hell-ride focused only on getting there as fast as humanly possible, no matter what! Fishing had become like a covert Special Forces operation. I would time myself on how fast I could get suited up and be on the water.

Without going into all the pathetic self-indulgent details of that particular pursuit of more and bigger trophy fish, I'll simply state that it was indeed a successful pursuit. Over the period of a few years, I caught thirteen more trophy fish ranging from five to eight and a half pounds and from twenty to twenty-six inches, and, to top it off, I did finally catch the "one that got away" — a massive nine-pound, twenty-seven-inch monster rainbow trout. But at what cost? Had I sold my soul to a trout-fishing devil?

CHAPTER 7

The Truth of It All

As many outdoor enthusiasts have pointed out over the years, there is a natural three-phase progression that those who fish and hunt go through. First, there is the "get-something phase." During this phase the individual is still learning the basics and the primary goal is to get those basics to work. The person who is learning to fish wants to catch fish and the person who is learning to hunt wants to successfully harvest game. The second phase is the "trophy phase," in which the individual is ready to learn more advanced techniques and passionately desires to fish or hunt for a more "advanced" critter. The final phase is the "philosophical/spiritual phase," where the sportsman (or sportswoman) has basically done it all and seen it all and now simply relishes the pleasure of the pursuit itself rather than the immediate fruit or focus of that pursuit.

These three phases mirror the phases that we go through in life, and there is much to learn and appreciate from each. When we are young and impressionable children, we are constantly learning the basics of life whether we realize it or not. We learn basic intellectual skills such as reading, writing, and arithmetic in grade school. We learn basic social skills by means of interaction with our family and friends. Our parents (hopefully) taught us the basics regarding manners, morals, and proper behavior. We may or may not have learned the basics of a particular faith tradition by means of going to church or Sunday/Bible school. We learn that there is a time and place for everything. The games we played and physical activities we enjoyed as children helped to develop our basic motor skills and social skills, as well as taught us the value of strategy, teamwork, and discipline.

These basic skills of life that we learn in our childhood are the foundation for the goals we strive to achieve for the rest of our lives. The basics that we excel in at an early age are usually the things we focus on developing as the years go on. As we grow and mature, we want to put these basic skills to the test in order to "get something." We may want to get on the football team in high school. We may want to be on the honor roll or do well at a speech meet. We may want to excel in the arts. We may want to make lots of friends and be the most popular kid in school. We may want to get into a particular college and intensely pursue a certain career choice. We want to get something in return for all the sometimes painful lessons we've learned in life thus far.

It's also in those early years that we learn the not-so-good basics. We learn bad language, bad manners, and bad behavior by means of observing the examples of others, sometimes even our parents. We learn how to cheat and manipulate people. Some of these not so good "basics" of life that we learn when we are young can negatively influence the rest of our lives just as prominently as the good ones. One of the things we discover when we're quite young is the power of a lie. We find out that we can get what we want, in one way or another, if we tell a lie. We can beat our friends at different games, stay home from school, and have people do favors for us and give us things all by simply not telling the truth. We find that we can do better on our homework, get good grades on tests, get people to like us, and make them think we like them all by telling a lie.

As we get older we find that we can get better prices on things, even get things for free, get ourselves into "elite" social organizations, attain a high-level job, and excel at that job all through lying. But we also find that we end up buying lots of things that we don't need and that don't even work because *we* were lied to. We find that the trust we had in someone or something has all been in vain and that our admiration of a particular role model or leader was all for nothing because of a lie.

As we go through life we are constantly subjected to untruths regarding what we eat, what we wear, what we drive, where we'll go on vacation and anything else we can think of. Certain lifestyles and moral decisions are advertised by way of the media as being good and noble, when, in fact, they are incredibly destructive and poisonous to the soul.

Fishermen lie about the size of the fish they catch (except for me, of course). Joggers lie about how far they can run. Golfers lie about the score of their game. Weightlifters lie about how much they can lift. Racecar drivers lie about how fast they can go. And, of course, in order to keep one little lie from being discovered, we have to tell more lies to cover up that one, and then more to cover that one. When it's all said and done, it can seem like everything in our lives and everything in our world is one big lie!

We ask ourselves, "Where is the truth? What is the truth? Why are we afraid to tell the truth?" Though all of us are talented and gifted in different ways and all of us can develop and unlock an incredible amount of potential within ourselves, the truth is that we will only reach and we will only attain a certain level regarding everything in our lives. And the truth is that we don't like that.

The truth is that some of us will never be able to look a certain way no matter how much dieting, exercise, or plastic surgery we get. The truth is that some of us will never have what it takes to reach a particular level of intellectual development and thus never get that super high-power career and be able to live the glamorous life we may want to. The truth is that no matter how hard we train and how much we practice, some of us will never reach that outstanding athletic achievement that we so desire. The truth is that it's selfishly wanting things that we know we could never get or never do on our own that makes us lie. And it's that same desire that makes us accept someone else's lie when we know better.

Jesus tells us that "the Spirit of truth . . . will guide you into all the truth" (Jn 16:13). It's that Spirit of truth that helps us realize that we are not perfect. We will never be perfect. We will never get all we want and be able to do all we want to do. We will always look a certain way and we will always be a certain way (to a point).

The truth is that that is how God made us. The truth is that he loves us no matter how we look, how smart we are, how strong or fast we are, how much money we have, what kind of work we do, how talented or creative we are, where we live or where we went to school. God, the source of all truth, revealed to us in his son Jesus, sends us that Spirit of truth so that we may see in ourselves and in others the truth of God's infinite love for us.

With God's love are no gimmicks, no slick sales pitches, no false advertising. He sees the truth in all of us, and he loves us and accepts us for who we truly are. He does not judge us for what we cannot do or do not have. He asks us to do the same of others. And when we accept that truth, we find that we no longer have to live a lie. When we accept that truth, we can truly appreciate and live out to the fullest the basics of life. When we accept that truth, we find that our "get-something" attitude has turned into a "thanks for what I have been given" attitude. But then comes phase two.

Phase two for the outdoor aficionado, the "trophy phase," in which an individual is ready to learn more advanced techniques and passionately desires a more advanced pursuit, is also mirrored in life. It's usually in our adolescence that we come to realize our particular gifts and talents on a deeper level. Perhaps we've begun to noticeably shine in the realm of the athletic, intellectual, or artistic, and we've become aware that with further development and a finer honing of our skills, we could quite possibly go on to achieve varying degrees of greatness. Inspired by this realization, we begin to sharpen our focus on a particular area. We begin to prioritize other areas of our lives around and in support of a certain goal. We begin to passionately learn more, train harder, think deeper and discipline ourselves more strictly in order to achieve that goal.

This more advanced pursuit that we engage in can simplify, intensify, motivate, and transform us into a different person, for the better or for the worse. For the better, we can learn a great deal of humility and allow that pursuit to enrich us. For the worse, an all-out focused effort to achieve greatness can fill us with arrogance and selfishness. Going back to the previous chapter, when I decided to single-mindedly pursue trophy fish, I experienced both the positive and negative effects. The positive is that I did go through a process of simplification, intensification, and motivation that eventually spilled over to other much more important areas of my life. I distilled a wealth of information and knowledge down into one operation manual that I kept filed in my brain for handy access. My focus on the goal that I wanted to achieve became excruciatingly intense. That process of simplification and intensification in turn motivated me to fish for trophy trout with an unstoppable determination. And reaching that initial goal inspired me on to aim even higher.

On the other hand though, I had "sold my soul to a trout-fishing devil" in that during the process of pursuing those trophy fish I had dissected the purity and beauty of what trout fishing is all about in order to self-indulgently, almost profanely, prove myself. Trout fishing was no longer a soulful journey through a mystical porthole into a new dimension somewhere between heaven and earth where I would experience the overwhelming wonder of God's creation. It had become a defiant, cold-hearted, bloodlust-driven race to hunt down and capture the king of the stream. I began to ignore areas of my life that were much more important. My school work, relationships, even my spiritual life all began to fall by the wayside as thoughts of catching huge fish overpowered my entire being. In the grand scheme of things, I only spent part of one day a week (if that) actually fishing, but that's all I thought about the rest of the week. It didn't matter if I was in the classroom, in the chapel, at someone's house, or anywhere else. My thoughts uncontrollably dwelled non-stop on catching gigantic fish.

It wasn't until after catching all those gigantic fish that the reality of what I sacrificed finally hit me. Yes, I felt fulfilled, redeemed, vindicated, and joyfully elated, but it was fleeting in the realization of how unbalanced I'd become in the process. Isn't it funny how we can want something so bad, and after we finally get it, say to ourselves, "Yeah, that was great, but now what?" We spend countless hours dreaming about something we want and burning thousands of calories just by thinking about it, and after the initial happiness wears off, it seems like no big deal. Such is the emptiness of our "trophy" pursuits in life.

Everybody pursues a "trophy" in one way or another, at one time or another. Some want a trophy house, car, or other material possession of some kind. Some want a trophy spouse or family. There are those who seek to hunt down a trophy career. Those trophy pursuits are always exciting, and again they can be very beneficial for us in regards to sharpening our skills and expanding ourselves, but when it's all said and done, the "trophy hunter" is never satisfied if he or she allows the corrupting power of greed to take over. There is always a bigger fish out there somewhere. There is always a more glamorous car or house. There is always a more high-powered position that one could attain. That need for more, for bigger and better things and more significant achievements can consume us. It can turn us into materialistic junkies who *have* to have the best of everything life has to offer.

The more one remains in that trophy-collecting mindset and the more one allows that greedy desire for bigger and better things to overtake them, the more they will become dissatisfied with what they have. The more one loses touch with the initial inspiration to do or achieve something, the more hollow and empty those achievements become after the adrenalin rush is over.

As a priest I see the ugly side of this "trophy" addiction all the time. I've seen "poor" out-of-work people on welfare drive up to a food pantry in a luxury SUV. I run into people who are basically allowing their children to go hungry so they can shop at the finest stores, have the nicest clothes, and drive the fanciest cars, while living in a rat-infested hell-hole eating food fit for the trash and piling up debt that even their grandchildren probably won't be able to pay off. Even if one can legitimately afford the best and most expensive things in life, one finds in the end that having all those "trophies" does not make up for one's lack of true self worth. When we try to define ourselves and our worth by what we have, we're in trouble. After all, the good book says that from dust we are and to dust we shall return (see Gen 3:19; Eccles 3:20). It's going after a "trophy" quality of soul that matters in the end.

Unfortunately, many folks don't begin to see the pointlessness of attaining mass quantities of finery until old age. When I go to visit the elderly and even the not so elderly in retirement and nursing homes, it's quite obvious they've grasped (sometimes by necessity) the concept of what really matters in life. In all cases, a houseful of material possessions that have been acquired over a lifetime are narrowed down to just a few things. And those few things in almost all cases are items that are reflective of the love in their lives. Pictures remind them of the love of their family. Religious items remind them of the love of the Lord. The few possessions they've held on to remind them of the true meaning and the priceless joys of their lives. They realize that the things they've perhaps taken for granted are in fact the true "trophies" in their lives.

Whether one allows that "trophy phase" of life to enrich them or corrupt them, the next phase, the "philosophical/spiritual phase," brings everything full circle. It's in this phase that one begins to get in touch with those initial inspirations. One begins to appreciate more than ever what they have been given, what they have truly achieved, and what they have learned. It's in this phase that a long-retired mechanic begins to work on his car with renewed enthusiasm. A veteran deer hunter will dust off his rifle and take to the November woods with really no intention of harvesting a deer. A well-seasoned athlete finds that playing ball with his kids is more satisfying than winning a world championship. After one has done it all and seen it all, what's left is the genuine enjoyment of an activity in its simplest and purest form.

It's in this final phase that a particular pursuit is no longer a catalyst for greatness, public recognition, or personal satisfaction, but it becomes an opportunity for wisdom, appreciation, and a doorway to get in touch with the divine. "Being" becomes more important than "doing." This, too, is a hard lesson to learn. In a "do"-oriented society it's easy for us to judge others and ourselves strictly by what we do. It's also easy to fall into the trap of defining our self worth by what we do (along with what we have). It's this mindset that has pushed many a good hardworking people over the edge into full-blown workaholics.

Once again, as a priest I see the destructive end results of this all the time. On an almost weekly basis I hear of marriages crumbling because a spouse is never around. I hear from kids who are convinced their parents don't love them because they're always working and they never spend quality time with them. Sure, their parents can give them anything their heart desires such as a nice first car when they turn sixteen, but they're never around to see them learn to drive. Of course, their parents say that they express their love by what they "do" for them and what they give or can get for their children. I've sat in on group-therapy sessions for teens that have attempted suicide, and almost every one of them came from a very well-to-do family. These kids seem to have it all. They're the kind of kids who would most likely be the envy of their classmates, yet the lack of loving contact with their parents and the signal that sends them can have a literally fatal impact.

On the flip side, I've visited with families who are hardworking, yet dirt poor, but who are the happiest people I've ever met. They've learned the value and worth of "being" for one another. Of course, I'm not suggesting here that wealthy families by default are going to be miserable and poor families are going to be happy. Obviously this is not the case. It's important to recognize that the true purpose, meaning, value, and satisfaction of our lives are found in living out our vocation.

A "vocation" can be defined as a calling from God to live out a particular way of life. Being a husband/father, mother/wife, son/daughter, priest/religious, and so on, are vocations from God. The purpose of a vocation is to live out to the fullest that self-sacrificing love of Christ, and we each are called to that in different ways. Most people don't care what their parents did for a living — they care that they had parents. They don't care if their dad was a magnificent lawyer — they care that he was a magnificent father. Most wives don't care if their husband is the best looking guy in the world — they care that he is the best husband in the world.

When we look back to those really significant events of our lives, we rarely can recall exactly what a particular person said or did. We recall that they were there with us when we needed their love and support. This shifting gears from "doing" to "being" is a hard one, but in time we realize its importance. It's in this final phase that we discover the truth of who we are and what is truly important in and about our lives. It's in this final phase that we come to the understanding that this truth is the very essence of the precious life God has given to each of us.

CHAPTER 8

The Sacred Hunt

"Bowhunting season" . . . those two words send shivers of excitement racing up and down my spine like a rat hurriedly scampering away from the light. Oh boy, just the mere thought of the autumn colors decorating the Missouri landscape makes my heart beat faster. To simply envision the golden leaves falling from the trees and the shades of green slowly evolving into a stoic gray beckons a silenced ovation for the joyful season of the harvest. Dreaming about what those exclusive aromas of the forest floor will smell like again stirs up a delicious taste from deep down within my soul. Imagining a dusky fall sunset reawakens a primal instinct that has been slumbering for months. The slightest thought of hearing the wind-driven rain and the crunching of leaves being blown along a rocky creek bed makes me want to trade in my Roman collar for a fur outfit of some kind and run through the woods screaming like a wild banshee, proclaiming that the time has finally come, the sacred hunt has begun! (I'm so excited just writing about this stuff that I can't even think straight now!)

I live for autumn. Not because of the great hunting and fishing opportunities, but because that season overhauls the very core of my being. I can't explain it, but something happens to me in the fall that seems to sustain me for the rest of the year. It's a time of spiritual healing and nourishment. As the natural world appears to be shriveling and dying during those autumn months, something within me comes to life and flourishes. I *have* to be out in the natural world as much as possible during the months of October, November, and December. I literally go into some kind of anxiety-driven withdrawal if I remain cooped up for too long during that time. I get sick. I start to die. I absolutely *need* nature at that time of the year. If I do not feed at the breast of mother earth throughout autumn, I grow sickly and weak like a malnourished pup whose fate is solid doom! For some unexplainable reason, my soul longs for God so intensely throughout the fall that it hurts. Ultimately, that desire to be in nature is the desire to spend quality time with God in a special way that only comes around for a few months each year.

Though I didn't seriously pursue hunting until my late teens, I have always been passionately drawn to it. When I was a kid I used to hunt (unsuccessfully) in the back yard for rabbits and squirrels with my homemade bow and arrow and anything else I could find to hurl at those fuzzy little critters. Isn't it curious how those instincts just naturally surface with no influence from anyone? I would spend hours trying to sneak up on the big fat rabbits that used to wreak havoc on my parents' garden. I would peak around the bushes and tiptoe up to within arrow-flinging range (which was about five feet) and try to hit the mark. But every attempt failed. If I actually got close enough to the ever-tamer rabbit, my clumsy bow wouldn't shoot the arrow fast enough or straight enough to do the job. I suspect that rabbit had a good laugh at me. But instead of watching cartoons of Elmer Fudd hunting down Bugs Bunny, I was busy trying to do the real thing.

Eventually, the time came that I was old enough to get a BB gun. My dad took great care in teaching my brother and me firearms safety and proper shooting technique. After polishing my marksmanship skills to a decent level of accomplishment, I began a new chapter in my childhood hunting career: backyard BB-gun hunting! I was now old enough to realize that I really shouldn't be shooting the rabbits and squirrels. I didn't want to eat them (not realizing at the time how tasty and nutritious they are), and anyhow I couldn't deliver a quick and potent enough kill with my particular hunting equipment. But the black birds were open for season! My mom hated black birds because they ate up all the birdseed that she put out for the song birds, and my dad unknowingly inspired me with stories of shooting them as a boy to keep 'em out of the chicken feed (or something along those lines).

Of course, my parents didn't know that I was actually hunting those big fat black birds. They were not too keen on the idea of me shooting my BB gun in the backyard where there was always the possibility of somehow missing and hitting a neighbor's window. But to me, that meant that I just had to be all the more careful, not to mention sneakier. In order not to be easily spotted by my parents, neighbors, or the birds, I decided that my best bet would be to hide in my room and shoot out of my slightly opened window.

The black bird-pillaged birdfeeder was hung in a dogwood tree about fifteen yards from my bedroom window. I'd stay crouched low on my bed with the muzzle of my BB gun slightly exposed. At last a big bully of a black bird showed up and chased off the other gaudy birds so he could chow down on all that delicious feed for himself. I slowly put my cheek on the dark wooden stock, lined up my sights, took a deep breath, released half of it, and squeezed the trigger. With a somewhat mighty gust of compressed air, my gun let out a muffled "Plaaatt!" The black bird tumbled off the feeder and flopped to the ground.

I casually left my room, trying my best to contain my excitement, and walked outside as if going to get some fresh air. I didn't want to make a commotion and alert anyone to my sneaky under-takings. I strolled over to my dead bird and admired the beautiful sheen of its feathers, while trying to ignore the glazed lifeless look in its eyes. Then it struck me: I had ended a life. I actually did kill something. I realized that this bird which was merrily flying around just moments ago would never fly again. I was responsible for this pointless loss. I certainly had no intention of eating it (although I did use its feathers to tie some flies), and even though their numbers did need to be thinned, I felt terrible that I was the one who took away this poor bird's life.

I knew that death was a part of life, but it was after shooting that bird that I realized that killing purely for the sake of killing is not a good thing. The paradox of hunting is that while death and killing is never in and of itself a good thing, it is an undeniable consequence, though not always the primary end result of the hunt. The primary end result of the hunt is a multileveled fulfillment.

There is the fulfillment of having put nourishing, healthy meat in the freezer by one's own efforts and not having had someone else do it, thus removing oneself from the reality that something must die in order for something else to live. There is the fulfillment of having successfully hunted and harvested a very elusive wild animal, which is an extraordinarily difficult and challenging thing to do. There is the fulfillment of taking an active role in being a good steward of creation: A certain percentage of particular animals must be "harvested" (a nice word for killed) each year in order for the species as a whole to thrive. Entire books have been written about the positive and necessary role that hunting plays in wildlife management. That being said, I'll leave further and more detailed study of the matter up to the reader. The purpose of this chapter is not a biology lesson.

Many anti-hunters say, "How can you look at that sweet little deer with those big brown eyes and want to kill it? How can you be so heartless and cruel? Haven't you ever seen Bambi?" Those are valid questions and they require a thorough answer. Regarding the question of, "How can you kill something so beautiful," what living thing is not beautiful? Everything that lives, by the very nature of its God-given life, is beautiful. A rose or flower that is cut off the stem (killed) only to be put in a vase to look at could be considered a tragic, pointless taking of life. A gardener or a farmer who raises vegetables or livestock does not do so for the sake of killing them, but the death of those beautiful, living animals and plants is essential for the sustaining of other life. The food chain is an undeniable reality. The greater is designed to consume the lesser.

To start from the top, we as human beings are omnivores. We are designed to eat a balanced diet of fruit, vegetables, grains, and animal products. There are certain vitamins, minerals, fatty acids, and amino acids that are vitally essential to our health and survival that can only be derived *naturally* from animal products. As with wildlife management, there has also been extensive research on this subject, so I'll again leave further study up to the reader. The purpose of this chapter is not a science lesson, but rather to give one quick example, as pointed out by Dr. Stephen Byrnes (ND, PhD, RNCP) in his article "The Myths of Vegetarianism":

> Today, vegans can avoid anemia (a fatal condition due to lack of vitamin B-12) by taking supplemental vitamins or fortified foods. If those same people had lived just a few decades ago, when these products were unavailable, they would have died.

Along those same lines, many of today's fad diets require artificial supplementation to get vital nutrients that the diets themselves do not supply. As the FDA has been saying for years, along with our parents, schoolteachers, and anybody else with a lick of common sense, a well-balanced diet and exercise is the key to staying healthy.

So, first of all, we see that we are designed to consume animal products and eat meat. If you don't accept that, take a look in the mirror and check out your canine teeth. They are there for a reason! And so it is, obviously, that an animal must die in order for one to consume it. Regarding the quality of meat, there is nothing as healthy as wild game meat. Deer meat, for example, is one of the healthiest of all red meats. With that being said, when was the last time you saw deer meat next to the pork chops and beefsteaks at the grocery store?

Besides the nutrition factor, there is the care and quality factor. When a hunter kills a deer (or anything else) for the dinner table, he or she knows that that animal was not subject to deplorable living conditions, steroids, growth hormones, or any other disgusting and unnatural treatment. The hunter is also obliged to take the utmost care in handling and processing that meat. Many hunters do all the butchering and packaging themselves as a sign of respect for that animal and in order to ensure that the meat will be of the best possible quality when it comes time to prepare it for the table.

Next, there is the satisfaction factor. As stated earlier, it is no easy task to harvest a wild animal, especially with a bow and arrow. It takes a great deal of knowledge, patience, and skill to be successful. For each animal that is taken, you can bet that hours upon hours upon hours have been put into making that hunt successful. There is great pride (the good kind of pride) in being able to have been self-sufficient and to have taken an active role in the food chain. We as a society have so far removed ourselves from the reality of this that it's almost humorous. Kids can't make the connection that the meatballs they just had in their spaghetti came from a real live cow, and their parents don't want to admit that Nemo (or your aquatic cartoon character of choice) had to die so they could have fish sticks for supper. We see nicely packaged meat in flimsy Styrofoam containers and have no idea where it came from and how it was handled, nor do we even know anything about that animal's life. In hunting and fishing, that knowledge is intimately known.

Every time a hunter cooks up and eats a delicious, nutritious wild game meal, the memories of the hunt, the respect, the humility, and the thankfulness for that animal's life is again experienced. When is the last time a cow or chicken was thought of so fondly or shown such dignity at the dinner table? And if that meat came from a trophy animal whose head probably graces one's wall, that animal will be revered as a celebrity among those in the hunting community. Trophy-book deer and other such animals of legendary status are cherished and admired for decades, even centuries. The memory of that animal lives on forever. The alternative is for it to die of old age, rot away in the woods and never be seen again, or to get hit by a car, expire from starvation and disease, or be killed by other predators who don't give a hoot as to how magnificent that animal may have been.

This respectful, intimate knowledge of a hunter's quarry leads to the final piece of the puzzle: ensuring a quick and humane end to an animal's life when it is killed. Here is what usually goes through a hunter's mind during the process of actually killing an animal: When a targeted animal finally comes within range and provides a clear opening for a well-placed shot, the hunter usually gets a massive flow of adrenalin. Sometimes that adrenalin is so much ("buck fever," as it's called) that the hunter shakes uncontrollably, freezes or can't even shoot. Once the hunter learns to channel that adrenalin into an almost superhuman focus, he or she realizes that this is the moment of truth. All the preparation, all the scouting, all the target practice, everything, comes down to just those few seconds. After the shot is made and the hunter has visually confirmed that it was a properly placed shot, there is another massive adrenalin flow combined with a sense of pure uncontainable joy in realizing that all that work paid off. I imagine it's what runners must feel when they've finally crossed the finish line after a long and excruciating race.

Then that paradox comes into play. Watching that animal drop dead (which usually happens instantly or within a few seconds) is never fun. It is sad to see such a beautiful animal's life end. But the realization that the hunt was successful and that the animal's life was taken with the utmost dignity, respect, and speed is a euphorically joyful feeling. There is a great sense of honor in having had the privilege to enter into the natural world and directly taken part in the cycle of life.

There is also the unfortunate reality of when things go terribly wrong and the hunter makes a bad shot, resulting in the animal never being recovered. I don't know any hunter who does not get almost violently sick to their stomach after the realization that they have made a bad shot on an animal. It is a horrible, haunting, gut-wrenching, almost tear-jerking feeling to know that an animal might suffer and die a not-so-quick death because of a bad shot. But still in the grand scheme of things, starvation, disease, or being eaten alive by other not-so-considerate predators, are the much more painful alternatives.

The reason that a hunter takes to the woods may be for a combination of these different factors, or it may be because of one in particular. Some hunt purely to put quality meat on the table (whether it be their own or other people's). Others hunt exclusively for the challenge and the tremendous satisfaction that comes with success. Some are in it primarily for the stewardship factor or because there is a very real need to thin the number of a particular animal for the good of the overall species and for the good of the land that supports them and other wildlife. Still others just enjoy being outside and relish the peace and quiet. No matter what one's primary motivation for hunting is, all of these factors are nonetheless of the utmost importance. An ethical hunter would never kill an animal for the sake of "sport" and not utilize the meat. Even "trophy hunters" who appear to be only after a big set of antlers or an exotic head for the wall do not waste any of the precious life-sustaining meat of an animal. Those who do are not hunters; they are disgraceful killers.

It is the process of actually hunting an animal (not necessarily killing it) that is so special. It is the sights, the sounds, the touch, the smells, and the tastes that one experiences during the hunt that makes it such a tangible yet ethereal endeavor. Most people who hunt get into it because of the reasons that were previously discussed. But underneath it all, the primary lure that draws many into the world of hunting (and fishing) is the solitude, the quiet, and the deep immersion and connectedness to nature. It's that intimate connection to the natural world that can in turn connect one more deeply to the spiritual. Admiration of the natural leads to admiration of the supernatural from which it was conceived and brought forth.

Solitude, peace, and quiet is a hard thing to come by for much of our "civilized" society these days. Everywhere we go we are sensually assaulted. Our daily experience is one of constant distraction. Sights and sounds emit nonstop from everything around us. We're jolted out of bed in the morning by that horribly abrasive squawking of the alarm clock or by some other offensive auditory stimuli. We hop in the shower and coat ourselves with all sorts of chemically infused smell-good, look-good goop and (if you're like me) administer several facial lacerations as the result of a rushed shaving job. We guzzle down our super-power caffeinated beverage of choice and maybe stuff some mega-processed food in our face if we have time, and then rush off to work. There we sit, in the morning rush hour with the radio filling our ears with the constant mind-numbing, gum-flapping chatter of deejays and music that sounds like the bellowing of a sow! The exhaust is thick in the air and the sound of honking horns, gritty diesel trucks, and the heavy booming bass of a half-deaf rap punk's stereo in the next car over becomes maddening! Meanwhile, we're on the constant lookout for those other half-asleep commuters who are bound to run us off the road, cut us off, or cause an accident somewhere down the line, only prolonging these purgatorial morning rituals.

When we finally get to work, our days can be filled with nonstop frustration. Certain co-workers aggravate us to the point of inspiring homicidal thoughts. Clients and customers who are impossible to satisfy keep making demands and lording their power of being a consumer over us. After all, "The customer is *always* right," aren't they? Phones ring off the hook. The pressure keeps building. For every one thing that gets done right, ten other things go wrong. You take three steps forward and ten steps back. A mountain is climbed, only to fall off the top and tumble back down to the bottom. And after the workday is done, the kids have to be picked up from school, taken to games, go to meetings, so on and so forth. The baby is screaming. The house is a mess. The grass has to be cut. There is no food in the fridge. AAAHHHHHHH! To top things off, when the hellish work week is finally over, the weekend goes by so fast that it almost seems like a humiliating mockery. We never seem to be able to catch our breaths. Peace and quiet? You must be joking! If only we had the luxury.

Throughout the centuries, many spiritual writers have spoken of the importance of silence, of being still. "Be still, and know that I am God," we hear in Psalm 46. God asks us to "be still" because he wants us to let go of all that stress, frustration, and aggravation. He wants us to spend time with him, just being with him and listening to him. In a nutshell, this is ultimately what prayer is: it is humbly being in God's presence and communicating with him.

There are various forms of prayer (both private and communal) that one can utilize. The *Catechism of the Catholic Church* addresses this very well, and it really does apply to Christians across the board, but it boils down to this: Essentially, prayer takes one of five forms.

First, there are prayers of blessing and adoration. In a blessing, God gives us something and we accept it. The prayer of blessing is our response to God's gifts. God blesses us and we in return bless God who is the source of every blessing. Adoration is our acknowledging that we are the creature and God is the Creator. It exalts the greatness of the God who made us and the power of Christ who saves us. Adoration is paying homage to God by means of respectful silence in his presence.

Second, there are prayers of petition, in which we come before God and humbly ask him for something. But, we do so always trusting and submitting to God's will.

Third, there is the prayer of intercession. In prayers of intercession, we pray on behalf of someone else; we ask God to do something for others.

Fourth, we have prayers of thanksgiving, in which we thank God for the many gifts and blessings he has given us. Thanking God also helps us to become more aware of God's love for us and helps us to realize how truly blessed we are. If you find yourself feeling depressed and drowning in self-pity, or if you become filled with envy or jealousy over what you don't have, just take a good look at what you *do* have and realize that there are lots of people out there who would do anything for what you've been so ungraciously taking for granted. While we sometimes agonizingly moan and complain about how our lives are so miserable, most of us have no idea how good we really have it.

The fifth form of prayer is the prayer of praise. Praise is the form of prayer in which we recognize most immediately that God is God. It's the joyful realization that we are loved by God.

All of these forms of prayer are expressed in many different ways and they are all necessary for our spiritual nourishment. But their purpose is to draw us into the presence of God so we can then be quiet, shut the heck up, and really listen to what he is trying to tell us.

It's not uncommon for the busyness of our lifestyles to creep into our prayer. Even while praying, we have the tendency to think that we have to be constantly doing something. We (or others) sometimes make demands on ourselves that we *have* to read a certain amount of Scripture each day, that we *have* to recite a certain number of certain prayers each day. We feel that we *have* to methodically crank out a particular series of spiritual exercises day in and day out. Let me make it very clear here that I am not dismissing or downplaying any of those things. All of those things are of the utmost importance. But when we are constantly, feverishly doing all of the talking, rambling on as fast as we can, we horribly fail to listen to God and to fully enter into his presence.

Peace and quiet is the heart of prayer. Throughout the gospels, whenever Jesus is preparing for some kind of ministry or a significant upcoming event, he always goes off to a "deserted place" to pray and rest. He asked his disciples (and invites us) to do the same. We have to spend time with God so that our time with others will be fruitful. It's similar to the cycle of resting and working. We can't work well unless we've had a decent night's sleep. In return, sleep doesn't come easy unless one has worked hard enough to be tired. Similarly, we can't get to know God if we don't spend time with him. We'll never get the grace we need to live out our lives in a healthy and holy manner if we never take time to come before the Lord and ask him for that grace. We have to *make* time for God. And a good portion of that time should be nothing more than placing oneself in God's presence and being still and silent.

You may be saying, "When the heck do I have time for all this stuff. I don't even have time to get a haircut!" The truth is that it doesn't take much time. A daily ten minutes of silence/prayer can do a person wonders. A half hour can seem like a mini-vacation. A whole hour can seem like heaven on earth in the midst of a chaotic day or week. Do what you can, but make sure you do it! Like any other serious relationship, a relationship with God takes commitment. So commit to some amount of time to spend with him daily. Go to that "deserted place" and spend some quality time with the Lord. *It'll change your life.*

You may be asking, "So, what and where is this deserted place?" A "deserted place" can be anywhere that is relatively quiet and free of distractions. Perhaps it's a quiet room in the house or maybe even the basement or garage. That "deserted place" might be the front porch or the back yard. It might be in a church, which, of course, is always the best place. That location might be in your car with the radio turned off. It might be in the shower or in the bathtub. It might be lying in bed. Heck, it might even be sitting on the ol' porcelain throne! It's up to you to find that place and to go there often.

Second only to church, my deserted place of choice is a tree stand. Those autumn colors that decorate the Missouri landscape are the backdrop for my personal meetings with the Almighty. Those golden leaves that fall from the trees, and the shades of green that slowly evolve into a stoic gray beckon a divine silence in my heart. Those exclusive aromas of the forest floor rise up like incense, praising the Lord and gently carrying my prayers heavenward. The dusky fall sunset opens my deaf ears to once again clearly hear the voice of God speaking in my heart. This is why the hunt is truly sacred.

CHAPTER 9

Not So Fast

As I GLANCED OUT the window and saw the leaves falling off the trees, my pulse began to quicken. Through the slightly cracked window on my left, I could feel a hint of the early autumn breeze. There I sat, held hostage in the classroom. Meanwhile, my mind raced with thoughts of getting to my tree stand. It was the first week of October and this was to be my first chance to get out and hunt. It was the bowhunting season kickoff, and there I was in the place I least wanted to be. I'd been preparing for that day for months. I'd been shooting my bow and sharpening my marksmanship skills, organizing my hunting stuff, mentally preparing different hunt strategies, going over various scenarios and frantically anticipating that magical moment that I'd be in the woods and have a deer or turkey come by my stand. I began to interrogate myself, "Would I be able to make the shot? Should I hold off for a bigger deer? Where would be the best spot to arrow a turkey? Will I be able to get to the check station in time? Will anyone be around if I need help dragging a big deer out of the woods? Do I have everything I need in my backpack?" On and on the questions kept coming.

Now with only a few minutes of class left, I was about to explode with a frenzied anticipation. Ten, nine, eight, seven . . . all right, when the bell rings, I'll run back to my room, take a quick shower, put on my clean clothes, and go. Six, five, four . . . okay, my bow is already in the van and everything that I need is packed up. Three, two . . . let's see now, it will take me forty minutes to get out to the woods, ten minutes to get changed and geared up, another fifteen minutes to walk to the stand, and so I should be in the tree by 2:00 P.M. which will give me plenty of time for a late afternoon/evening hunt. One . . . blast off!

Before the bell even rang, I was halfway out the door and back to my dorm room. I threw my books on the desk and executed my prepared plan perfectly. I was on the road in ten minutes flat. I could barely stay on the asphalt as I shoved a peanut butter and jelly sandwich in my mouth and washed it down with some canned iced tea. I was so excited to finally be at that moment in time. My left hand gripped the steering wheel tight and my eyes were fixed on the road as I listened to my favorite pre-hunt music. Once I got off the highway, I carefully raced through the back roads. Being true to my pre-hunt ritual, when I reached the last stretch of road, I turned off the stereo and spent some time thanking the Lord for this opportunity and asked his blessings upon the day. As I pulled off the road onto the patch of gravel where I always park, my nerves calmed down a little. I'd reached my destination, and I realized that this much anticipated moment had now become a reality.

I quickly went through the process of changing into my hunting clothes, putting on my boots, double checking all my gear, rubbing cedar branches all over me to cover my scent and spraying myself down with some human scent neutralizer as an added extra precaution. I quietly closed the back door of my van and began to make my way to the tree stand. Still experiencing that first-day-of-the-season rush, I walked with an exceptionally brisk pace. It was downright hot that day and it didn't take long for my temperature to start to rise. As I felt that first bead of perspiration start to form on my forehead, I became alarmed, "Oh no! I'm starting to sweat!" Once that first bit of sweat starts, it's all over, at least for me. It's like turning on a faucet. I knew within a few more minutes I'd be drenched in sweat from head to toe.

Of course, the realization that I was sweating only added to the anxiety of the whole situation and made me sweat even worse! For those of you who aren't familiar with the finer points of deer hunting, especially bowhunting, controlling one's scent is of the utmost importance. Many hunters go to extreme, almost comical measures in attempting to control, eliminate, or disguise their human scent. This, of course, is because a deer's nose is its most powerful weapon. Long before a deer may see you, it can smell you. And if it smells you, it's gone!

As I felt my clothes get heavier with soaked up sweat, the whole hunting season seemed to pass before my eyes. "What if the monster buck of the woods gets a good whiff of me and bolts off into the next county never to set foot on this property again? What if the wind shifts and carries my scent throughout the entire woods, stinking up the whole place and spooking every creature that walks and crawls?" My imagination ran wild and I began to envision every deer within miles rushing out of the woods in a panicked mass exodus, driven away in terror by my scent as if it were a deadly gas. As I was consumed with these troubled thoughts and the realization that I was now sweating like a big fat cook in a hot little kitchen, I began to rush to my stand in order to get there as fast as possible so I could hose myself down again with some scent neutralizer spray.

Speeding through the woods with all sense of caution thrown to the wind, I crossed the creek with all the care of a crazed wild horse. As a result I jumped up and ran off four turkeys. Moments later, as I stomped through a cedar thicket, I heard that disheartening familiar sound of deer blowing their alarm whistle,

"Vooshh. Voooooshh!" As I looked up, I saw their white tails waving me goodbye. Needless to say, I was a bit upset. After finally making it to my stand and spooking every animal in the process, I de-scented myself again as best I could, climbed into my tree stand and tried to make the most of what was left of my fabulous first hunt of the season.

As my breathing slowed down and I began to relax a bit, I began to notice a strange and unpleasant feeling in my gut. Those peanut butter and jelly sandwiches were not sitting all that well. The pressure in my gullet grew to a painful ache, and just when I thought I could take no more, the pressure was released suddenly by means of what was possibly the loudest and most malodorous flatulence I have ever produced! My vision of every deer running out of the woods to escape a toxic gas was now becoming a reality!

After my stomach settled down and I was finally able to relax, I got into bowhunting mode. My heart rate began to slow down, and my body became still and motionless. My intense sweating ceased and I found myself drying out and cooling off. With every passing minute my senses became sharper. My eyes began to focus intensely on each and every detail of my surroundings, looking for the slightest twitch of an ear or flick of a tail. My ears began to hone in on and amplify even the slightest of sounds. The only thing moving, ever so slowly, was my head as I scanned the territory back and forth on constant red alert, looking and listening for deer or turkey.

It really is an amazing phenomenon when one's senses take over so intensely while the body is so still. It's equally amazing how exhausting it can be. Some people think hunting is a lazy activity, where one just sits around or leisurely strolls through the woods and shoots an animal that just happens to be standing there as if waiting to be shot. Nothing could be further from the truth, especially when bowhunting. During the hunt, one's entire being becomes a super-sensitive alarm system. It can be extremely mentally taxing and unbelievably exhausting. One's powers of concentration and focus are pushed to the edge and beyond. Sitting in a tree stand, totally immersed in the woods, motionless, yet *internally on fire*, is as close as it gets to having some kind of an out-of-body experience. One becomes keenly and uniquely in touch with one's awareness of awareness. One's senses become hypersensitive. Sounds are not just heard, they are felt. They radiate throughout the entire body. Sights are not just seen, they draw a response from the depths of one's soul. The fragrance of the forest becomes intoxicatingly euphoric. The feeling of the wind, rain, or snow on one's skin (in moderation) evokes a hypnotizing sensation. During this process of immersion into the natural world, one truly realizes and experiences the distinct, unified nature of oneself — physically, mentally, and spiritually. The body, the mind, and the soul each have a particular role, each separate from the other, yet still working as one unit.

After sitting or standing totally motionless for some time, one appreciates how significant it is to do something as simple as open and close one's hand or move one's arm or leg. That transition from thought to action, potential to activated potential, is something we never give much thought to, but how incredible! It's amazing the control and sensitivity that we have both mentally and physically. It's just a hint of what we are capable of as human beings on a much larger scale.

So there I was, finally in full bowhunting mode, hoping to hear that wonderful sound of the leaf-rustling footsteps of a whitetail or the raking of feeding turkey. My eyes searched the backdrop for moving shades of black, brown, gray, and white. It's interesting to note that the first thing a prey animal notices (besides scent) is movement and sound. If a deer notices any kind of movement that cannot be identified, or a sound that is unnatural, you guessed it — gone in a flash! Likewise, the hunter must be on the constant lookout for sights and sounds, but natural ones. A predator has to be able to recognize the slightest movements and sounds of his prey while also not spooking it with his own movement and sound. As the afternoon turned into evening and I sank further into that meditative bowhunting zone, I began to realize that my earlier bombastic ordeal of getting to my tree stand had ruined my hunt. Not a creature was stirring except for a few squirrels, birds, and an ominous bat that kept circling my tree as the sun went down.

Relaxed and refreshed, yet disgusted and worn out, I got down from my perch and went back to the van. As I drove home, I repeatedly kicked myself in the rear for my serious lack of stealth and my frivolous hurry. Of course, this wasn't the first or the last time I spoiled things from being in a frantic rush. Learning to be quiet, to slow down, and to methodically plan every movement is a lesson I'm still learning. Many of the old timers say that when you're walking through the woods, stalking an animal or just making your way to a particular location, you should not take more than a few steps per minute. Take a step or two, slowly and carefully look around, listen, plan your next few steps, and then take them. At such a pace it may seem like it would take hours to get to where one is going, and it does take a lot more time, but it's amazing what you start to notice.

When I started to really slow things down, a whole other world was revealed to me. I began to pay attention to and actually notice things like slight animal tracks, droppings, rubs, scrapes, bedding areas, feeding areas, travel corridors, and lots of other signs that I had been looking for but missed because I was always in such a hurry. I began to notice things that really didn't have anything to do with hunting, but that were simply wonderful to behold. I began to notice the pleasing earthy scent of specific trees and plants. I began to discover how much life, big and small, was all around me. I started to appreciate the sound of the dew dripping off the leaves in the early morning breeze. I began to be joyfully consumed and overwhelmed by the raw manifestation of the creation of God. It was something that I hadn't paid close attention to since I was a child discovering the beauty of nature for the first time.

When I took the time to pay attention, evaluate, appreciate, and learn from such things, my hunting success increased significantly. For myself, I define hunting success in part by simply being able to locate and observe wildlife without disturbing it. Of course, it's great to be able to close the deal and actually harvest an animal that one is pursuing, but as we've already learned, hunting is not about simply killing an animal. When one tallies up the hours spent in the woods and the actual number of animals harvested, it's quite obvious that a hunter spends the vast majority of his or her time hunting, not killing. And as I hope the reader is learning by now, there is a lot more going on during the process of hunting than meets the eye.

This hard lesson of learning to slow down is something that all of us can benefit from. We miss out on a great deal when we rush through life. When we are in such a hurry to accomplish or experience one thing or the other, we overlook the tremendous blessings that are right before us. When we constantly try to "keep up with the Joneses," we fail to appreciate the things we have. We fail to truly appreciate the love of family and friends. We fail to be thankful for the food, shelter, employment, health, and basic necessities that we take for granted. We fail to experience the priceless joy that comes from the simplest things in life.

How often we fail to recognize those simple joys because our priorities are so terribly confused. We franticly race through life to achieve our immediate goals, but at what cost? Is making extra money so we can buy extra things that we probably don't need and will soon forget about anyway really worth sacrificing time we could have spent working on things that will matter for all eternity? As a wise young family man once pointed out, "I'll be an engineer for the next thirty years, but I'll be the father of my children for all eternity." How much is it worth to throw away what could have been quality time with one's spouse or fail to be more active in the lives of one's children because something else seemed more important at the time? At what cost do we stab our friends and coworkers in the back in order to advance ourselves and put more money in the bank?

As a priest, I encounter lots of people who have lost a loved one. And it doesn't matter if the deceased is a child or someone very elderly, the response from the family is always the same: "I wish I would have spent more time with him or her. I wish I had told him or her this or that. I wish I would have paid more attention when *(fill in the blank)*." Most people would do anything and would pay any price to regain a lost opportunity or to have more time with a deceased loved one, especially if death was untimely. A lot of folks mentally and emotionally torture themselves because they were so concerned with things that, in the face of a tragic loss, added up to absolutely nothing except a second look at their flashy car or a compliment about their nice house or stylish duds.

No one except God knows when, where, or how we will leave this world. In the meantime, we're all on that journey through life headed toward eternity. We can be in a frantic rush and never appreciate or even notice the God-given beauty of our lives, our relationships, and our world, or we can learn to slow down and savor every step. We can hurriedly stumble from one paycheck to the next, from one meaningless, fleeting, self-indulgent pleasure to the next, from one fancy new material possession to the next, and crash and burn as we blindly search for what we've scared off and what we've failed to see along the way. Or, we can learn to open our eyes, ears, and hearts in a new way and experience to the absolute fullest the countless God-given gifts, joys, and blessings that are all around us.

CHAPTER 10

The Spirituality of the Outdoors?

A PHRASE THAT I'VE BEEN hearing more and more lately from different people that I meet is this: "I'm not a religious person, but I am a very spiritual person." Spirituality is a popular thing these days. It seems that almost everybody is after some sense of the spiritual in their lives. Even many of our pop-culture superstars claim to practice some kind of spirituality. Some say that riding a motorcycle and getting tattooed from head to toe is a spiritual experience. Others state that various forms of exercise or listening to certain styles of music are for them of a spiritual nature. Of course, I tell people that fishing and hunting can be a spiritual experience. The activities that we as individuals find to be "spiritual" are just as different and diverse as we are from one another as a people.

So what, then, is spirituality? Is it comprised of random, though unique, activities that we each engage in on some conscious or semi-conscious level to nourish the "spiritual" nature of ourselves? Are there norms or universal characteristics of spirituality that connect and relate them all to one ultimate expression?

In our modern day, the word "spirituality" has in many cases become a term for anything that is even vaguely related to a religious expression, but without the religious belief or disciplined practice. I heard a talk (recorded in the '60s) given by the late great Archbishop Fulton Sheen in which he addressed this matter. He pointed out the trend that over the years when the Church would let up on a particular practice, the secular world quickly adopted it as its own. People stopped saying the rosary, and then it became a popular piece of jewelry. The use of incense and candles became less frequent, and then people began to use them in their homes. The habits (dress) and clothing of particular religious orders and communities were worn less and less, then suddenly fashion designers began to imitate those designs more and more. As the belief in angels and even the recognition of the demonic began to fade out of Sunday sermons, the next thing you know it becomes the subject matter of million-dollar movies. In just the last few years, Gregorian chant has become popular again, but the meaning, purpose, and message of the music is totally overlooked by the secular world.

Spiritual *things* appeal to people very much, yet the true meaning and purpose of those things is often not even recognized. Many people really like the idea of meditating in candle light with incense burning and listening to relaxing music, all the while gazing into a crystal or whatever else, basically because it makes them feel good. Perhaps it helps them to relax, to focus, to relieve stress, or to get the creative juices flowing.

In all honesty, I think the primary motivation for those who claim to be spiritual, but not religious is, "What's in it for me? What will I get out of it to make *me* feel better?" And it's almost comical how some will pick and choose different practices and different beliefs from different religions, yet belong to none. In the Catholic Church, we have what we call "cafeteria Catholics," who like to pick and choose certain doctrines and practices and flagrantly disregard the rest is if they were handled by the grubby mitts of a diseased monkey.

There are also those rooted within mainstream churches that attempt to apply elements of other religions to their own as some sort of spiritual supplementation. I was on a retreat once where our retreat director (for the day) wanted us to listen to some bizarre New Age chant music and pray in the direction of the four winds while in the chapel, a Catholic chapel (for those of you who aren't Catholic, that's a big no-no). Cooking up these theological and spiritual stews is unfortunately not all that uncommon, especially within certain religious communities (which out of charity I won't name). This is not what true spirituality is about. Making up our own little religions based on what we like and don't like does not make us spiritual; it makes us terribly confused and severely misguided.

We have to keep in mind that God chose to reveal himself and his plan of salvation for us in one particular way (as found in Scripture), in one particular person (Jesus Christ), for all people of all time. Even many who are active members of a particular church can get caught in the trap of seeking entertainment and warm, fuzzy, feel-good stuff instead of true worship. And when they get tired of the music, the pastor/minister, or the community, they jump over to a different church or parish.

Instead of coming to Church asking ourselves, "What's in it for me?" we should ask, "What was in it for him (Jesus)?" He suffered and was put to death so that we might live. He was made the object of hatred so we might learn to love. He experienced unimaginable pain so that we might experience the unimaginable joy that comes with the forgiveness of our sins. Without his sacrifice, there is *nothing* in it for us. No amount of incense or candles, uplifting music, beautiful decorations, flashy vestments, lovey-dovey, feel-good homilies, or anything else matters one bit. It would all be for our own shallow entertainment.

We go to church to thank God for that sacrifice through which we have salvation. We go to church to praise God for the joy that comes from his forgiveness. We go to church to worship God for his love that knows no bounds. And it's through the power of the Holy Spirit that we do these things. Just as the power of the Holy Spirit descended upon the apostles at Pentecost and transformed their lives so that they could go out and spread the Gospel message throughout the world, so, too, it is the Holy Spirit that inspires us to live out and share the Gospel message. It is the Holy Spirit that inspires our worship and makes our music and decorations and everything else we do in church so powerful, so meaningful, and so beautiful. It is the Holy Spirit that helps us give thanks to God, to praise God, and to worship God with all of our might.

The true meaning of spirituality is to live a life inspired by the spirit, in accordance with the spirit — the one and only spirit — the *Holy Spirit*. And so the initial question remains: Can riding a motorcycle and getting tattooed from head to toe, engaging in various forms of exercise, listening to certain styles of music, hunting, fishing, or anything else genuinely be an experience of the spiritual? To answer that question, one has to ask oneself if the activity in question is ultimately geared toward experiencing the inspiration of the Holy Spirit. Again, certain "spiritual" activities may make us feel good; they may help us to relax, focus, or whatever else, but they will not necessarily draw us into the realm of the truly divine.

To use the example of hunting and fishing (though anything applies), these can be spiritual activities at times, and at other times they are not. Kicking back on the river bank, drinking beer, and watching the sun set while fishing for catfish certainly is relaxing, but usually it does not significantly change my relationship with God or others. Meandering down a scenic trout stream gently casting to those vividly colored fish often takes my breath away, and the beauty of the whole experience always overwhelms me, but it usually does not instill within me a more disciplined sense of virtue. Sitting in a tree stand, uniquely in tune with all of my surroundings, truly becoming one with the natural world, and successfully harvesting a game animal is an activity that brings great satisfaction, but it usually does not deepen my understanding of the mysteries of God.

Now, the key word in all of this is *usually*. There are, however, times when fishing on a big muddy river does significantly change my relationship with God and others because of the inspiration of the Holy Spirit. There are times when, because of the Holy Spirit, trout fishing does instill within me a more disciplined sense of virtue. There are certainly times during those long tree-stand vigils that my understanding of the mysteries of God are deepened by the inspiration of the Holy Spirit. If not, I obviously never would have written this book.

The Holy Spirit is at work all the time, but he really goes to work when the power and inspiration of the Spirit is consciously evoked. Therefore, when an activity is consciously offered to God, specifically as a catalyst for the working and seeking of the Holy Spirit, it does in fact become "spiritual." Catching a mud-belching, mean-faced catfish, *in and of itself*, is not spiritual. Neither is flinging an arrow at a deer or coercing a trout into taking a fly. Neither is getting a tattoo of a skull-faced weirdo or standing on one's head chanting some nonsensical gibberish. Nor is lighting a bunch of candles, burning some wild smelling tarry goo, flailing one's limbs in a bizarre dance, or contorting oneself into horrible positions while staring at the sun and rendering oneself blind! What *we* do does not make an activity spiritual. What *God* does to us through an activity does.

The other important factor here is discerning if God is truly at work or if we are only dabbling in idolatry and summoning forth the self-made god of our own selves, inspired, not by the

Holy Spirit, but by our inflated ego. In order to tell if a certain activity or experience was inspired by the Holy Spirit, one only needs to analyze the fruit of that activity or experience. The biggest mistake we make is judging the worth and validity of a "spiritual" experience by if it (yet again) made us feel good. If it did, great, but that's not necessarily the work of the Holy Spirit.

It is also important to note that we do not have to always be the one to seek the Spirit by means of one method or the other. It is quite often the Spirit that seeks us. It is very common for the Spirit to work profoundly in our pain, suffering, personal disasters, and unfortunate mishaps. We learn a lot when we are in a situation that *makes* us surrender our pride. We sometimes only hear God's voice when we are *forced* to shut up and listen. At times we only come to sense God dwelling in our hearts when we are *forced* to be still. Sometimes it's only by means of suffering that we get the motivation to do something that we should have done a long time ago. Unfortunately, it's often not until we're really down and out, or in a horrible situation, that we finally realize the destructive nature of certain things in our lives.

It is not uncommon for us to act as spoiled children and expect God to work on our terms and to do what we want, when we want, how we want. And if he doesn't meet our exacting demands, we dismiss God as unloving, uncaring, and deaf to our prayerful pleading. Sometimes the good Lord reminds us that indeed we are the hard, dirty old clay and he is the potter who with love, tenderness, and sometimes a good kick to the rear end makes us into something beautiful and quite profound.

Without a doubt, there are plenty of times when a true encounter with the Holy Spirit does make us feel great immediately. Most often, though, the Holy Spirit challenges and inspires us to do things that are not necessarily going to be a joy ride, but it is those things that will ultimately set us free from sin and help us to enter into a deeper, more loving relationship with God and others. In a nutshell, if a particular "spiritual" experience or activity does not strengthen one to live out to the fullest the love of God and inspire one to spread the Gospel message, then it is not of the Spirit. It still may be good and make one feel great, but so will drinking a bunch of beer and eating a big juicy steak, along with a huge baked potato with sour cream, shredded cheddar cheese, those little bacon bits, several tablespoons of real butter, and a whole bunch of chives! *Mmmmm!*

CHAPTER 11

Monster of the Monastery

DURING THE SUMMER of my first year in the seminary, I was introduced to what would become my personal spiritual sanctuary. This location is by no means "my" personal refuge, but it has become a unique wellspring of renewal that has refreshed my soul like no other place on earth. This particular place is a monastery located in deep southern Missouri called Assumption Abbey. For those who may not be familiar with what exactly a monastery is, it is basically a chunk of land where monks live, pray, and work. These are usually places set apart from the hustle and bustle of modern life. They are settings of relative silence and tranquillity, but also of tremendous zeal and rigor. A monastery is a sacred place where one leaves worldly pursuits behind in order to journey inward to the heart of the soul.

The monk travels the inner path in search of God. As one of the monks from Assumption puts it, "A monk is a man who practices dying as a way of life. A monk dies to his egoism, his self-deception, to the illusions about who he should be and what life is all about that his upbringing and his culture has lain upon him; he dies to his compulsions and to his raw emotional responses to people and to situations." He concludes, "A monk is also a man who practices coming to life and living. At the same time that he is dying, he discovers an exhilarating freedom for life and for love. He discovers who he really is, and that discovery is not different

115

from the discovery of the true God and the destiny of the universe, the God who is love, the Father to whom all are being drawn into one."

Contrary to the stereotypical preconceptions one may have about monks, they are certainly not troubled misfits who couldn't hack it in the "real world" and thus plunged themselves headlong into a ritualized life of escapism. Monks are some of the wisest, holiest, knowledgeable, hardworking, and joyful folks I've ever met. A monk's life is a combination of self-sustaining work and prayer. They get up very early (some at 3:00 A.M. or earlier) and offer their entire day as a prayerful sacrifice for the world. Isn't it good to know that every day there are holy people out there who have dedicated their entire lives to pray for all of us! Pope John Paul II referred to monastic prayer as the "backbone" of the Church. Their prayers affect us all.

From my first visit to this particular monastery, I knew there was something very special about it. I ended up there in the first place because I was supposed to spend a few days with some of my seminary classmates as part of an initially much dreaded monthlong retreat. When I arrived that first time it was under the cover of darkness. We got sidetracked that afternoon, and as a result we didn't begin the four-hour trek to the monastery until the evening. As the sunlight slowly faded and the amber Midwestern sky turned into a mysterious clouded Prussian blue, we found ourselves more and more deeply immersed into the towering pine forests that seemed to overtake us like an earthen army as we drove deeper south. When darkness was upon us, all I could see was the greasy black asphalt lit by the bug-smeared headlights of the old Ford van that carried us along the hilly Ozark terrain.

At the direction of our navigator, we suddenly veered off the blacktop onto a gravel road, which eventually ended at the monastery gate. When I got out of the van, the first thing I noticed was the darkness. Due to the cloud cover that night, there was no moon or starlight peaking through. It was monumentally pitch black. As the dome light went out from within our well-worn vehicle, I could not see my hand in front of my face. I had never experienced anything so dark, so richly devoid of any light in all my life. Yet, in the midst of this divine darkness, I felt something I'd never quite felt before. I could actually feel a holiness radiating around me. I could feel that I was at a very special place. I felt the sweet presence of God more intensely than I had ever felt it before.

It's that radiating, overpowering, sweet presence of the divine that has been bringing me back every year from then until now. It has become a place of spiritual healing, of emotional rejuvenation, of physical relaxation. It is a location that positively affects me in an indescribable manner. It makes me whole. It puts back together the broken and charred remains of my being in these soul-shattering times.

The first actual day of my initial visit was equally as profound as the first night. The blackness of night had given birth to a new morning, and when I woke up that first day I found myself gazing out the window upon a vast wilderness nestled in the Ozark Mountains. I quickly went outside and walked around the immediate grounds to have a look. I tingled all over as my eyes traveled from hilltop to hilltop. The stillness and quiet was pleasantly unreal. I quickly discovered that this is a place of breathtaking beauty and sacred solitude. As I ventured around the outlying area, I found that there were several streams nearby carved within the ruggedly handsome landscape. As I strolled along, I came to a spot where a mountainous rocky cliff stabbed straight down into the pure rushing water, creating sort of a natural cathedral atmosphere. It's that spot that truly has some kind of supernatural power over me. When I'm there, I feel as if our loving God is holding me in the palm of his hand. I feel complete. I feel a hint of the purity with which we all were created at that initial moment that God decided that we should be.

I've been incredibly blessed over the years to have been able to travel throughout a good portion of the world. I've seen many wonderful things that in all humility I realize many folks only dream of seeing. It's through the charity and generosity of others that I've been able to experience and visit many places of renowned marvel, and I am eternally grateful for those opportunities. But still, without hesitation, I can honestly say that this one particular spot on the monastery grounds, that natural cathedral area, is for me the most beautiful place on earth. It is my true spiritual sanctuary. For me, it is the center of the universe.

Being surrounded by all that holy, natural wonder, the fresh air, and the clean fish-filled waters of those Ozark streams, well, it naturally gets my outdoor-lovin' blood a-flowin' fast! You can bet that it didn't take long for me to find myself knee deep in the pure aqua with a fishing rod in hand. Let me point out (believe it or not) that fishing is never my initial reason for going to this place, but it is an added extra. As always, it's a great catalyst for simply enjoying the area, taking a break from retreat activities, and just plain having a good time. Not to mention, I've had several life-altering inspirations while wandering down those streams talking with the Lord and looking for fish.

Fast forward now to May 24, 2003. This was to be the most important day of my life. That was the day, after eight years of study, that I was to be ordained to the Catholic priesthood. In preparation for that grandiose event, I decided to go to the monastery once again to make a retreat for a few days in order to mentally and spiritually prepare myself. One particular morning of that retreat, I made my way down to the creek. I had no initial plans to fish; I just wanted to take in the sights and sounds of my favorite place on earth. As I walked along the creek I was quickly reminded of why I came. The cool, clean water seemed to wash away all my troubles and apprehensions. The surrounding Ozark Mountains lifted my thoughts to greater things. Just being there at that moment was, as always, a foretaste of heaven. As I aimlessly strolled along, all the while immersing myself into the captivating beauty of this special place, something in the water caught my eye. Up ahead, in the next bend, the water was boiling and thrashing wildly. I quietly snuck up around the other side of the bank to have a look. As I approached I saw the creek plugged up with spawning long-nose gar.

I've had plenty of experience with gar over the years while cat fishing. But this was different. It was a rare primal dance, savage in appearance, prehistoric in nature, yet wonderful to behold. They were darting back and forth, diving up and down, snapping their teeth, and coursing through the water as if preparing to feed on a dead hippo.

After watching this ritual for several minutes, I could no longer take it. I had to go back to my van and get a rod. As with any serious fisherman, I never leave home without at least one rod and some tackle. All I had in the back of the van was a fly rod and some light fly-fishing gear. Without delay I rigged up the ol' Deadly White Jig on the heaviest tippet material I had, which was a shabby piece of weather beaten six-pound test line. I went back to the creek bend and started casting into the slug of fish. It was actually quite similar to fishing for spawning salmon in Alaska, but here I was in southern Missouri in the middle of nowhere.

Most of these fish were of average size, some bigger, some smaller. As anyone who has ever fished for gar will attest to, you're lucky if you land one out of every ten you hook into (using traditional tackle). The same held true that day. I'd hook one, he'd get off. Hook another, have him on for a few seconds, then he'd get off again. It's very difficult to drive a hook into that long, slender, boney mouth. I was able to land a few here and there and it was incredible. Catching those big toothy rascals on a short five-weight fly rod was an absolute blast!

Just when I thought I'd had all the fun I could handle for the moment, something again caught my eye downstream. In the crystal clear water I noticed a huge object moving upstream toward where I was fishing. As it got closer and I realized what it was, I froze in shock. Here before me was the largest, creepiest, wildest looking reptilian beast of a fish I'd ever seen! This was no doubt the alpha gar! The king of the creek! As my buddy from Arkansas would say, it was a "gargantuan gar of seismic proportions!" I've caught tons of alligator gar over the years and I know they can get huge. The long-nose gar gets big, but I'd never seen one this big.

As he moved into my casting range, I calmed my nerves as best I could and cast my fly to him, humbly offering this aquatic hulk a tasty, hooked delight! Without delay he darted forward and my fly disappeared into his cavernous mouth. Needless to say I wasn't really expecting that to happen. It was one of those moments that is just too good to be true and you can't imagine that things are working out so perfectly. In an instant I set the hook as hard and as carefully as I could. The monstrous fish turned and headed downstream. There are no words to describe the feeling of a fish the size of your leg bolting downstream as you try to fight him with a tiny fly rod. David and Goliath indeed! And to try to describe what it was like to see this whale of a fish actually make several aerial leaps is even more difficult.

After twenty minutes of very, very carefully trying to slow down this torpedo, I was able to finally wear him down enough to drag him up on a sand bar. When he was safely on shore, I just stood there in complete awe of the size of this fish. I got out my measuring tape and scale to see just how big he was. He weighed in at 25 pounds and was 45 inches long. Knowing that no one would ever believe this tale without proof, I had to get a few pictures. I hung my camera from a tree limb, hit the timer and got a few snapshots. I couldn't quite get a grip on him, and he kept snapping at me with that long snout full of razor-sharp teeth, so I had to lasso him with a belt in order to hold him still for the picture. After that, I set him free. What begun as just a peaceful stroll turned out to be the most savage battle I've yet to experience in fresh water. The old boy scout motto held true once again, "Always be prepared!"

After that fantastically exciting experience, I went back to the monastery chapel to thank the Lord and joyfully reflect on what just happened. As I thought about similar occurrences of great things happening when least expected, I realized that those situations always seem to happen when I'm completely spiritually in tune, when I'm "in the state of grace," as we Catholics say. When I'm in the state of grace, I feel faith, hope, and love dwelling in my heart with great abundance. I sense the virtues of courage and patience empowering me to live a holy life, to avoid sin, and to deal with troublesome ordeals in a healthy, productive manner. Life still dishes out the same old punishing predicaments whether one is in a state of grace or not, but that "amazing grace" that God offers us is very real. It is very powerful. Without it, we crumble under the stress and pressure of life. Without it, those troubled times that come our way will beat the tar out of us and leave us a mangled mess for the vultures of corruption and self destruction to pick us apart like a pungent, sun-baked, offensive-smelling road-killed opossum!

For those who may be unfamiliar with the term, "grace" is a free and undeserved gift that God gives to us to live out our vocation. As discussed in a previous chapter, a vocation is a calling from God to live out a particular way of life. A vocation is the role in one's life that really matters. It's our true purpose. For all of us, our primary vocation is to imitate the self-sacrificing love of Christ, but we do that in different ways: as a spouse, a parent, a sibling, a priest, a religious brother or sister, etc. With each of those vocations there are particular challenges and struggles that come with striving to live it out to the fullest. And it's the grace of God that gives us the strength that we need to do so. Grace draws us into a deeper friendship with God. It sanctifies us. It helps us to develop in the ways of virtue and leave behind the ways of vice. Grace assists us in transforming our will to be in accordance with God's will.

When we are in the "state of grace," we are spiritually in tune. Grace enables our conscience to become more active in guiding us through those confusing and tempting paths that we some-times travel in life. Grace makes us much more aware of things we should be doing and things we should be avoiding. When one is in the state of grace, it is as if God directly takes you by the hand and leads you through life. Grace is like a legal steroid for the soul (with no side effects). It is a supercharged nitro blast of spiritual energy and confidence. It's like a stiff dose of "miracle grow" plant food for the soul. It's a direct lifeline to the Almighty!

That joyful and magnificent feeling that comes from being in the state of grace and that phenomenon of being spiritually in tune flows over to all areas of one's life. When I'm in the state of grace I sleep better, live healthier, exercise harder, pray more devoutly, go out of my way to be more charitable to others, and seek to share the love of God with all I meet in one way or another as best I can. When I'm in the state of grace I stay much more focused on the things in my life that really matter. I keep my priorities straight. As a result, I also enjoy free-time activities much more. And, of course, this purifying, energizing, sanctify-ing grace also seems to take over when I'm fishing and hunting.

When I'm fishing in the state of grace, fish (sometimes very big fish) just seem to hook themselves to the end of my line with wild abandon (much to the dismay and unbelief of my fishing buddies). When I spend time in the outdoors with that awesome grace running through my heart and soul, great things just seem to happen all the time. It's as if God opens up the sky and dumps a heaping truckload of blessings down upon me. Even if the fish are not biting, being in the state of grace just seems to make everything around me glow with the bright light of God's love.

Along with hooking into that jaw-dropping mammoth gar, I've caught several other trophy fish on occasions that transpired much like that one. The grace of God just seems to emit out of my heart, travel through my fishing rod, shoot down the line, and attract the fish to my grace-covered fishing lure or fly. When I'm out on the water on those grace-filled days, it's almost as if I can just think about getting a bite, and sure enough it happens. It never ceases to amaze me as to what God will send my way on those kinds of days. That sense of being spiritually in tune is feedback from the Lord that, indeed, everything is spiritually in tune (at least for the moment). On those blessed fishing outings, it's as if God is saying, "I love you" with every fish I catch, with every songbird I hear, and with every wonderful sight I behold.

Of course, the other side of the coin is not being in the state of grace. When I find myself coated with the stain of sin and my soul blackened like a delicious red snapper, everything becomes a lifeless, fruitless burden. Disaster seems to strike like a mercilessly fierce lightning bolt, screaming down from a ravenous dark cloud of doom! God seems to be a million miles away. Everything is covered in a shroud of black. I feel awful, weak, strung-out, unhealthy — in a word, miserable. Disaster strikes while in the state of grace as well, but it's all the more crippling when that grace is not present.

Such is the nature of sin. Sin destroys the life and the grace of God within us. It severs that lifeline. It cuts off our friendship with God and negatively affects our relationships with others. Sin is a very serious matter. When we choose to live a life of sin, we choose to reject God. And when we separate ourselves from God in this life, that separation continues in our eternal life — we go to hell.

God, of course, is not the one who sends us to hell. We send ourselves there by choosing to refuse the love, the mercy, and the grace that he offers us. That lifeless, fruitless, disastrous, blackened, awful, weak, strung-out, unhealthy, miserable feeling that comes from sin is what I imagine hell must be like. Hell is being separated from the presence of God forever, and there is nothing worse than that; but again, it's something we freely choose.

There is a certain passage from Scripture that has troubled people for decades. That passage is where Jesus says: "If your right eye causes you to sin, pluck it out and throw it away; it is better that you lose one of your members than that your whole body be thrown into hell. And if your right hand causes you to sin, cut it off and throw it away; it is better that you lose one of your members than that your whole body go into hell" (Mt 5:29-30). If we took this passage literally, we'd live in a world filled with half-blind, limbless people. The point Jesus is trying to get across here is that we should take whatever means necessary to separate ourselves from the things that separate us from God. We have to be aggressive in avoiding the things that become an occasion of sin and that lead us into temptation beyond our control.

Avoiding that "near occasion of sin" is the key to avoiding a particular sin all together. If watching certain things on TV, listening to certain music, going to certain websites, reading certain publications, or being around certain people or places becomes a source of temptation, then those "occasions" of temptation, which lead to sin, have to be "cut off" or they will ultimately cut us off from God.

The effort that we sometimes put forth regarding cutting ourselves off from sin is like trying to cut through a tough old piece of meat with a flimsy plastic knife. It may work, eventually, but it's not very effective. The kind of effort Jesus challenges us to put forth is like using a two-handed, head-chopping meat cleaver!

A lot of times we don't take our sinfulness all that seriously. And, of course, our culture doesn't help the matter much when the things we are trying to avoid are celebrated in the media, thus chiseling away at our awareness of the gravity and seriousness of sin. It's tough to avoid temptation and sin. Anybody who thinks that Christians are weak-minded, do-good pushover sissies have no idea what being a follower of Christ is all about. Just look at some of the martyrs of the early Church. It's unbelievable the things they endured for the sake of Christ and the Gospel message.

Taking a stand for what is right, aggressively avoiding sources of temptation in the face of a sin-addicted world, having the courage to do the right thing, and striving to imitate that self-sacrificing love of Christ is no walk in the park. It can become a daily crucifixion. It's a far cry from the undisciplined, hedonistic, materialistic philosophy and lifestyle of much of our culture. It takes an incredibly determined and strong person to effectively and aggressively cut themselves off from sources of sin. It takes a tremendously courageous person to tell the truth, to stick up for what is right, and to act in accordance with the will of God. It takes a fearless warrior of a person to love someone and pray for someone who only hates them in return.

If the strength, determination, courage, and genuineness of the Christian were to bodily manifest itself, we Christians would look like an army of people like Arnold Schwarzenegger in his prime! But we don't. Our strength is not of our own making. It is a gift from God. As St. Paul said, "For when I am weak, then I am strong" (2 Cor 12:10). When we realize that it is only through the grace of God that we are empowered to live a fruitful, holy life and avoid sin, it is then that we realize just how much we need that grace. Without it, we remain a laughable mockery of what we were meant to be as children of God. We become "whitewashed tombs" (Mt 23:27), as our Lord put it: pretty on the outside, but filled with dead men's bones!

CHAPTER 12

Seasons of Change

A UNIQUE CHARACTERISTIC of the dedicated outdoors enthusiast is that he or she feverishly looks forward to the changing of the seasons and the distinct opportunities each season provides. For some, springtime brings to mind the thunderous raspy gobbling of Mr. Tom Turkey. It summons forth visions of new glossy greenery emerging from the dormant soil of Old Man Winter. For others, it's the proper time of year to dust off the fishing gear and take to the waters in hot pursuit of one's fish of choice. Soon after, the sweltering days of summer offer the chance to take it easy in the shade and cast some awful-smelling rotting filth in the water in hopes of catching those wily catfish. Still others are more attracted to things like float trips on cool spring-fed streams and early-morning bass-fishing extravaganzas during those hot, humid days.

When fall comes around, many become hopelessly obsessed with visions of whitetails and flushing pheasant dancing in their heads. Others dream of tempting hungry brown trout with their favorite autumn fly-chow. Winter separates the men from the boys as some retreat to the fireplace, sip scotch and conjure thoughts of warmer days, while others defiantly brave the bitter cold in search of a late-season buck or a frosty rainbow trout. Each season has its own charm. Each season can have an exclusively different meaning and appeal to each outdoorsman. We all look forward to different things at different times of the year, but we all look forward to something. With each passing season, the sportsman grows, matures, learns more, and puts newly acquired knowledge and theories to work.

As for myself, I, too, am always learning and trying new things, but not a whole heck of a lot really seems to change from season to season. I fish and hunt basically the same places, I seem to catch about the same number and similar quality of fish each year, and I have about the same rate of success when it comes to most of the game I hunt. The one exception is bowhunting for deer. Things seem to change each and every season. Drastically! And boy have I learned some tough lessons out in those deer woods!

I took up deer hunting around the time I turned twenty. Though I had a lifelong interest in archery and always enjoyed shooting, I never had a place to actually go and hunt deer with a bow, or even a gun, for that matter. All that changed during my first year in the seminary when I befriended a fellow outdoor fanatic (and now brother priest) who taught me the basics of deer hunting and let me hunt on his family farm. After that first initial (though unsuccessful) season, I was hooked. I became infatuated with deer hunting like some crazed, lovesick lunatic who can't stop thinking about the nonexistent woman of his dreams. I ate up deer-hunting information like a starving fat-faced hog who'd been aggressively filling its acidic gullet with soggy slop fit for the bowels of hell! I craved whitetail knowledge with the same sweaty addictive desire of a three-pack-a-day cigarette smoker having some kind of a horrible nicotine fit! Man, oh man, I was hooked good!

By the time the next year's archery season came around, I had acquired an arsenal of deer-hunting knowledge to try out. Being that it was all book knowledge, I didn't have a grasp on what was fact and what was fiction. I didn't know what tidbits of wisdom were of actual value and which were fodder for the intellectual garbage dump. Another thing I did before the season opened up was to find some closer and more accessible places to hunt. I did my homework and found a wealth of huntable public land that I (and probably countless others) didn't even know existed. These places were so abstractly located that most of the area locals didn't even know of their whereabouts. I made several scouting expeditions to one place in particular and decided that I would focus my efforts on that piece of land for the season.

This location consisted of about two hundred acres of swampy river-bottom terrain. There were deep, cavernous creek beds carved throughout the land that seemed to be formed by great cracks in the earth's surface. There were steep, hilly ridges and low, musty valleys jammed shut by all sorts of thick brush and unkempt tree growth. There were tons of deer signs and yet little evidence of hunting pressure.

It was also a very creepy place. It was easy to get lost. It was a mysterious dwelling that seemed to go through some kind of metamorphosis with each footstep I took. During those scouting missions I would always feel as if some kind of a mutant beast was watching me, waiting to pounce on me and rip my head off with the raging fury of a dog trying to pass a peach pit!

October 1 finally rolled around, and I went to hunt this new and rather disturbing spot for the first time. I arrived at around 5:00 A.M. and got my things together. It was a dank, dismal morning and there seemed to be a hint of something terribly evil in the air, as if Satan was lurking around in the foul stench of this stagnant river bottom. I began to slowly make my way to a spot that gave testimony to regular deer travel. It was a location that connected a nearby bean field to the thick, damp woods. As I settled into a crude ground blind that I had constructed previously, I began to relax. Everything was still and quiet.

The starlit outline of my surroundings radiated a sullen blue aura as the sun began its ascent. All of a sudden I heard what sounded like a tank coming through the woods. Branches broke and leathery leaves were stomped into the muddy ground under the furiously dominating footsteps of what sounded like a very large four-legged beast. It was too dark to make out what it was (though I new it had to be a big deer), but it was certainly in a hurry to get where it was going.

The sun finally came up, and after hours of not seeing any wildlife activity at all, I decided to call it a day. Before heading back to my vehicle, I checked out the area where I heard all the predawn raucous. My suspicions were confirmed as I admired a large set of fresh deer tacks that were crisply stamped along the edge of the creek bed.

I hunted that area whenever I had the chance throughout the season with similar results. It seemed that on every outing I'd encounter deer in the dark and absolutely nothing during daylight hours, except for a few yearling does on one occasion. It was frustrating, but still just great to be able to be out there hunting. When it was all said and done, it was a completely fruitless season, except for just getting some in-the-field experience. I began to wonder if perhaps these primarily nocturnal deer were the reason nobody hunted this piece of land. Those deer were like vampires. At the first glimpse of the sun they'd scamper back to their reclusive daytime hideouts as if the light would singe the hair from their bodies and melt their bones! It was weird and troubling. It was disturbing indeed.

By the time my third season came around I realized that I still had a lot to learn. I still had not even seen a deer during legal hunting hours, at least not one that was close enough to take a shot at. I went back to the drawing board and studied up on things like favorite deer foods, bedding areas, travel corridors, funnels, scrapes, rub lines, scent control, and tree-stand placement. That year I spent much more time scouting and really doing my pre-season homework. That was also the year that I began to start hunting on a particular piece of private land that would become my all-time favorite hunting ground.

When the first day of the season was once again upon me, I found myself fifteen feet up in a sturdy oak tree overlooking a well-used deer trail that led to a thick grassy area with lots of white oak acorns nearby. To top that off, it was right alongside a little creek bed that was littered with rubs on the surrounding trees. I was right smack dab in the middle of everything I'd been looking for. As I sat in the predawn darkness and gazed heavenward at the brilliant stars above, I felt a tremendous sense of accomplishment and joy. As I smiled from ear to ear, I realized that I had made it. Here I was actually doing something that I only dreamed about for so many years. As always, it was great just to be there.

All of a sudden I was shaken from my special little moment as I heard powerfully heavy footsteps coming toward me. I knew it had to be a deer, and a big one at that! It sounded like it was splitting stumps in half and crushing the heavy creek rocks into a fine powder as it came my way. The sound got closer and closer, and when it stopped it was right below my stand. Still unable to make anything out, I froze. I heard some grunting and sniffing around, and then the steps continued. As soon as it was directly down wind from me, it let out a loud "Voooooosh! Voooosssh!" I was busted! He smelled me! He was gone in an instant.

I saw many deer that year, but mostly I'd see them running away, giving me the white-tailed wave goodbye, or if I did see them from my stand they were way too far out for a shot. Right before the opening of gun season, I went out for a final bow hunt with a buddy at his friend's farm. They set me up in a tree along a fence line that overlooked a bean field. They told me that the deer come out into the field every evening like clockwork. I was excited and bursting at the seams with the notion of actually being able to take a shot at a deer, finally.

Sure enough, when the sun began to slowly go down, the deer filed out one by one from the woods and came out into the field. And I'll be darn, they were headed my way! My heartbeat accelerated like a nitro-powered dragster. I began to shiver and shake with excitement as the adrenalin started to unleash. The lead doe was working her way over to me. Step by step, inch by inch, she kept coming. She'd take a few steps, stop to eat, sniff around, look back and forth, and then take a few more steps. She was in no hurry. As she closed in to within bow range, I began to get ready, as best I could, for the shot. I was shaking so violently that I could hardly get my bow in position. At last she was within 25 yards. I drew back my bow with all my quickly diminishing might and held the trembling sight pin on her vitals. I released the arrow and watched it zip right underneath her and plunge into the dry soil.

I missed! Holy Moses, I missed! After two and a half seasons of not even seeing a shootable deer, after all those miserable sleep-deprived mornings and evenings, after all the time I'd invested in studying deer and after all the preparations that were made to get to this one fleeting moment, I missed! I was stunned speechless. I was literally sick with disappointment.

In the fallout of that disheartening event, I decided to hang up the bow for a while and brake out the trusty 30/06, as firearms deer season was about to begin. I hunted the opening weekend with some friends at their farm. It was my first time in the stand with something that I could effectively shoot more than forty yards, and I was sure my luck had to change. As the sun came up that first morning of the hunt, I heard shots ring out from all around me. It sounded like a war zone. Yet I was still seeing nothing. Hours passed, and there was not a deer to be seen. I was getting very upset. I was beginning to feel like God had it in for me. After all, all this time I'd been pleading with him to send a deer my way. Isn't it funny how the good Lord gets blamed for everything that doesn't work out exactly how we want it?

It was now almost 10:00 A.M. and I was frustrated beyond belief. Just as I was about to start another round of complaining and blaming the Lord for making things so aggravating, two does stepped out from behind some cedar trees and began to come my way. When I had a clear shot, I raised my shaking rifle and tried to steady the cross hairs on her vitals. I pulled the trigger. After the recoil punched me hard in the shoulder and the smoke cleared, the deer was still standing there, just looking around with a rather confused look. I missed again! Good God Almighty, I missed again! What the heck was going on here!?

I quickly cycled another round in the chamber, put the crosshairs back on the mark, and this time, slooooowwwwwllllllyyyyy squeeeeeeezzzzzzzed the trigger. As my rifle let out another roar I saw a red mark appear behind the deer's shoulder. She took off and quickly toppled over in mid-run. I did it! I finally did it! I waited awhile just to make sure she had expired and then I got down from my stand. I excitedly followed the thick, short blood trail to where my deer lay. When I got up to her, I realized that this was one tiny deer. It made Bambi look like a monster! Nonetheless, I was elated. I had finally gotten a deer. I spent some time thanking the Lord for this wonderful creature and apologized for getting so upset with him. Everybody made fun of me for shooting a deer that wasn't much bigger than a good-sized dog, but I didn't care. I was proud of my little deer. Plus, those little ones are much tastier and a heck of a lot easier to drag out of the woods!

Even though getting that first deer was a very special event, my heart was still set on getting a deer with my bow. Bowhunting was (and still is) my primary passion when it comes to hunting. It didn't take long for the satisfaction of getting that first deer to wear off. I soon found myself back in the woods with bow in hand trying to successfully finish out the second and last half of the archery season. Once again it was a painstakingly fruitless ordeal. I didn't see any deer at all. Once the firearms season was over, all the deer just seemed to vanish. By the time archery season had ended, I found myself disgusted and filled with contempt. I had another failed season under my belt. I had (ungraciously) almost completely forgotten about my first deer since it wasn't taken with a bow, and all my prayers and pleading with God for a successful hunting season seemed to be in vain. Why was God being so mean to me? Why wouldn't he answer my prayers? Was I asking for too much?

As a people of faith, we ask God for many things on a regular basis. Probably not a day goes by that we don't ask God for something. When we are children, we ask God for things like a new bike or a pet dog (or a big deer). We see God as sort of a Santa Claus figure who is there to give us all sorts of gifts, especially the gifts that we want. In our adolescence we have a tendency to think of God as a helpful guardian. We beg God to spare us from embarrassing situations with our peers and plead with him to get us through one troubling ordeal after another.

In early adulthood, we often go through a period of making God prove himself to us. We start to really question many things about our faith and about God, and we want him to perform all sorts of self-proving mini-miracles. When and if we successfully make it through that stage, we begin to see God as a divine personal assistant. We seek his help in finding work or getting started with a successful career. We ask him to help us find a potential spouse, to grant us children, a happy home, and things of that nature.

Toward the end of life, many see God as a great healer. We ask God for comfort in the midst of failing health. We ask him for peace within our families. Ultimately, we ask God to help us be prepared for when he calls us home.

Throughout our lives, we pray for lots and lots of different things. When we look back, some of those things probably seem a bit ridiculous to us now. Many of those things we are probably glad we never got. It's probably a good thing we didn't get a motorcycle for Christmas when we were six years old. Maybe it was God's plan that we ended up doing something really stupid and embarrassing when we were in high school. Perhaps it taught us a valuable life lesson. It very well could have been God's will that we were never able to get the attention of that person we had a crush on. That job we never landed could have been the best thing to ever happen to us.

Lots of seemingly bad things happen in our lives for good reasons. And sometimes those bad things happen for no good reason at all. But no matter what happens, we have to trust in the Lord. We have to learn to echo the words of Jesus, "Not my will, but thine, be done" (Lk 22:42). We have to believe with all our hearts what we learn in the Gospel: That God loves us, and if we knock, the door will be open. If we ask, we shall receive. If we seek, we will find. But the key is that what we *want* and what we *need* are two very different things. We *want* lots of things. We actually *need* very little. God will always give us what we need, and he may even give us what we want from time to time. But it will always happen on his terms, on his time, and according to his loving will.

I wanted to have a successful archery season. I wanted to take a deer with my bow. I wanted things to work out exactly like I had planned and hoped. I wanted God to be a divine gift-giver, helpful guardian, personal assistant, and healer all at the same time. I wanted God to be my servant. The truth be told, I wanted to be God. I wanted to be in charge. I wanted things to happen when, how, and where I wanted. I had forgotten that all I really needed was his love. All I really needed was an activity that allowed me to enjoy the beauty of his creation and spend some time in prayerful solitude. All I really needed was one little deer to put some meat in the freezer and share with my friends and family. All I really needed was some healthy recreation. All of those things he gave me in abundance; but, as usual, I was too blinded with ingratitude and selfishness to realize it.

The frustrations and trials of that season were nothing compared to what the next one would bring. As the start of the new season began, I had several good tree-stand locations picked out, and I decided that no matter what, this season was going to be successful. I had methodically planned and prepared for every possible aspect of the hunt. I utilized every tactic and technique that I could possibly think of in order to make things happen that season. This had to be it!

Sure enough, that year I saw lots of deer from my stand locations. Every time I hunted, I had an encounter with deer. I saw deer of all caliber, including a real monster buck! But intertwined with these significantly improved hunting experiences, every single time something went horribly wrong. Every time I had a deer come by my stand I just couldn't get a good shot. The deer was either just a bit out of range or there would be limbs or brush in the way. On other occasions, the deer would stop right behind a tree that was just big enough to cover its vitals, again obstructing a good clean shot. Still, at other times, the deer would not be at the right angle or would be walking too quickly and wouldn't stop to offer me any possible chance. To top that off, on a few other occasions my buddy (who had just started hunting) would come by my stand for one reason or another and unintentionally scare off the deer that were closing in on my area.

Everything that could have possibly gone wrong that season did go wrong, and then some. I was bombarded with terrible weather conditions. On two occasions, I came down with diarrhea right when I got into my stand. I contracted a malicious case of the flu combined with a skull-crushing ear infection right at the beginning of the firearms season (I still hunted, though — never say die!). On another occasion, my bow fell out of the tree and broke. At one point I missed yet another deer, this time a buck. I had to let several good deer walk during the gun season because of new restrictions that were implemented on one of the places I hunted. It was just one thing after the other. As a result, I began to sink into a terrible bad luck-induced depression. And, of course, I once again blamed it all on God. As the season from hell came to a close, I was tortured by all the lost opportunities and the mistakes that I had made. But I realized that this was reflective of a phenomenon that takes place on a much more encompassing scale.

I think it's safe to say that all of us are haunted by mistakes we've made. There are things that we've all done that we regret terribly. There are sins that we've committed that we just can't seem to forgive ourselves for. There are lost opportunities from the past that flash before our eyes when we least expect it. All of these things can really do a number on us. And even if those sins and mistakes happened years ago and we've reconciled our differences with God and one another, those things can come back to haunt us and make us feel terrible. It's usually when we encounter or witness someone else making that same mistake that we start to relive that experience all over again. And the more we dwell on it, the more damage it does.

We can end up badgering ourselves mercilessly, asking, "Why did I ever do that? Why didn't I do this or that? What was I thinking?" The more we interrogate ourselves and beat ourselves up over mistakes of the past, the more we tear down our self-image and self-confidence. And the more we tear down our self confidence, the more we break down as human beings. It's not uncommon to torture ourselves over the sins of our past so much that we start going right back down the road that led to those sins in the first place.

We can start to convince ourselves that we really haven't changed. That we can't change. That the progress we've made in a particular area of our lives has just been a matter of good luck. It's interesting to note that our memories can be one of the greatest occasions for sin; we realize that we've committed a particular sin in the past, thus realizing we're capable of it again. It's this demonically inspired negativity that then starts off that domino effect of spiritual and personal self-destruction.

Once we commit that first little sin as a result of our weakened and wounded self-image and guilt, we begin to quickly let down our guard and begin to fall into more serious sin. The devil whispers in our ear, "Well, you've done that; you might as well do this." And before we know it, we're down for the count. The devil uses that tactic of guilt over past sins because he knows how incredibly effective it is to get us to commit future sins. He knows that it is in direct opposition to the true freedom and healing that Christ offers us. We hear in the Gospel that, "No one who puts his hand to the plow and looks back is fit for the kingdom of God"(Lk 9:62). In other words, when we are journeying with Christ toward the kingdom of heaven, there is no turning back if we want to make it to our destination. Obviously, there is a lot to learn from our mistakes and from looking back through history, but when we dwell on it to the point that it keeps us from going forward, we're in trouble.

The good news of the Gospel is that the sins of our past, if reconciled, are just that — reconciled and in the past. The good news is that the forgiveness of God, which was purchased for us by the blood of Jesus, washes away our sins, no matter how serious. God offers us a clean slate, no matter what we've done. When we constantly look to the failures of the past, we lose hope for the victories of the future. And truly accepting the forgiveness of God is what gives us the grace to achieve, to embrace and to realize that victory. Sometimes it's hard to realize that God has and can forgive us because we don't *feel* forgiven. It's important to keep in mind, though, that the guilt we experience because of our sins is not necessarily a bad thing, because it reminds us not to do those things again.

That was a hard lesson to learn. After the smoke cleared from that disastrous season, I again came to the realization that in the midst of all this hunting stuff, all I really needed was God's love. All I really needed was an activity that allowed me to enjoy the beauty of his creation and spend some time in prayerful solitude. All I really needed was some healthy recreation. This time that lesson set in for good. And wouldn't you know it, smashing success soon followed.

CHAPTER 13

Sweet Success

It was an unseasonably chilly October morning as I made my way along the edge of a moonlit hayfield. Ah yes, that magical first day of the archery season had arrived, and it could not have been a more perfect morning. Putting into practice the lessons learned from the past several seasons, my approach to the tree stand was very slow and very quiet. I carefully eased through the freshly frosted remains of the now bare field. When I finally reached the other side, I decided to stop and remain still for a few minutes before entering the thick woods that led to my creek-side stand location. The air was radiating a tingling icy mist, as if the morning had been chilling inside a meat locker. There was something special looming in the air. I had never felt more alive and so filled with joy to simply be there at that time and at that place. I knew this was to be the day.

After I spent a few moments surveying the ground-dwelling stillness, I began phase two and made my way through the thick, twisted jungle that led to what was becoming my favorite stand location. Moving with a broken cadence to disguise my human gate, I successfully snuck through the brush and crossed the creek without spooking anything in the statuesque morning twilight. The only thing left to do was climb up into my skyscraper tree stand.

Being that this particular stand location is along a creek bed and at the bottom of a steep ridge, I had to place my stand way,

way up there (thirty feet or so) in order to be out of view of the deer that may (and do) travel along the ridge. I tied my bow to the hoist rope, climbed the tree, strapped myself in, readied my gear, hoisted up my bow, and melted into the silence as I awaited the autumn sunrise.

My eyes adjusted quickly to the surroundings as the full moon bathed the woods in a pearly lunar sheen. I wasn't in the tree for more than ten minutes when suddenly I heard those distinct footsteps of an approaching early morning deer. Ten yards in front of me, a nice buck materialized out of the slender trees that kissed the edge of the creek bed. It was a majestic sight that I'll never forget. He moved slowly and proudly as he came right toward me and stopped to sniff around under my stand. The large crown of antlers he wore on his head reflected the moon beams and gave off a stunning sapphire blue glow. The fur on his massive body appeared to be brushed and groomed to perfection. Not a hair was out of place. It appeared that all my efforts to remain scent-free paid off as he casually walked on after giving my area a thorough olfactory inspection.

My heart teemed with delight after witnessing such a beautiful sight. I gazed heavenward, smiled, and said, "Thank you, Lord." That encounter alone would have made my season. As a result of the previous year's disasters, I was now hunting with purified intentions. The only thing I really cared about was enjoying God's creation and simply spending time in a place I loved. I did all my homework, put in the hours of preparation, and thoughtfully planned strategies for my hunts, of course, but how things worked out was ultimately up to God, and I was satisfied with that. I made a conscious decision from that season on to simply surrender the time to him. I was hunting for God, and if a deer happened to come along in the process, great. And that's what happened as soon as the sun came up.

Just when it was light enough to see my immediate surroundings, I heard a soft grunting sound coming from somewhere in front of me. Having done a good deal of pre-season study on deer vocalizations that year, I pulled out my grunt call and gave some soft grunts back as if to say, "Hello. I'm over here. Won't you please have a drink of water with me?" I heard approaching footsteps followed by more grunting. I grunted back again. The footsteps got faster and closer. I put away my grunt call and prepared myself to shoot, knowing that the moment of truth was at hand. My heart raced, my breathing quickened, and the adrenalin was starting to flow. I knew it was about to happen.

I stayed calm as a huge doe appeared and stepped out from behind a tree, giving me a perfect twenty-yard shot. As I drew back my bow I noticed that I wasn't shaking and out of control like those occasions in the past. I was focused. I was able to channel that adrenalin into an unbreakable concentration. As I put my sight pin behind her shoulder, everything else around me disappeared. All I could see was my pin and the spot where I wanted the arrow to go. There were no distractions. Everything seemed to be happening in slow motion as I gently released the arrow and watched it fly straight through the deer's side, hitting the mark perfectly. She bolted back down the path from which she came and disappeared in the thick brush. Then the aftershock of adrenalin kicked in and I shook like the leaves in the tree I sat in. But it was a great feeling. I knew I did it!

As my hands continued to tremble with those sweet victory convulsions, I lowered my bow and put all my gear back in my pack. I stayed in the tree for a good thirty minutes since, due to the thick foliage, I was not sure if she dropped or where exactly she was. When I got down, I went to where she was standing when I made the shot and quickly discovered my frothy blood-covered arrow. I began to follow the blood trail, which took me on a very short journey around to the other side of the brush in front of my stand. She did not go more than twenty-five yards. It was a quick, humane end.

I knelt down next to the big doe and thanked the Lord for this wonderful creature. As I ran my hand across her course, brown fur, I was filled with respect and awe for this magnificent animal. I sat down next to her and remained in a reverent silence for some time. I had done it. I finally successfully harvested a deer with my bow. After I paid my respects, I knew I had some serious work to do. It was a short but heavy drag through the woods, across the creek, and to the edge of the hay field. I dressed out my deer, drove the van over and loaded her up in the back. The sun had only been up for forty-five minutes. I excitedly showed the deer to the landowners and shared with them details of the morning's hunt. Then it was off to the check station. As far as I know this was the first deer taken in the area that season. None of the check stations were even open yet, and when the one in the next county did finally open, I was the only guy around. I praised God and shouted with joy as I then drove over to my parent's house to share the excitement with them and to start butchering the deer.

Five days later I found myself back in the same stand, but the morning passed with no deer sightings. Around 11:00 A.M., I decided to partake in a delicious peanut butter and jelly sandwich. I hung up my bow, sat back in my cozy tree stand, and started to delight in the simple and incredibly satisfying pleasure of my fanciful culinary production. As soon as I started munching away on the cold but hearty sandwich, something caught my eye. I slowly turned to look over my shoulder and there on the ridge, moving as quietly as a church mouse, was what I initially thought was a horse with a huge wicker basket stuck on his head. But it was no horse. It was *the* buck of the woods! My jaw gaped open, allowing a fistful of mashed up PB&J slop to ooze out of my mouth like a careless cow who's spit up her grassy cud.

My heart started to beat wildly with excitement as I slowly eased into a standing position. Ever so cautiously I tried to reach for my bow. As soon as I moved a muscle, the mighty buck spotted me (or at least something about me) and went back from whence he came. Wow! It was awesome to view such a majestic creature! To even see an animal of that caliber in the wild is a rare treat. Whenever time allows, I spend the entire day, sunup till sundown, in a tree stand. I see a lot of action during those times that are supposed to be the worst for hunting or even seeing deer. And every year I have an encounter with a big buck when I least expect it, usually when I'm eating lunch in the middle of the afternoon or while I'm going through my backpack for something.

About ten minutes after that monstrous buck vanished, two smaller bucks came down the same path. They stopped at the exact point the big guy did, but then turned and started heading right for me. I got in position for a shot, and before I even had time to think about getting nervous my arrow was on its way, in direct route to the buck's heart.

It hit the mark, and after a few wobbly steps, he dropped right before me. I couldn't believe it! After all those deer-less seasons I had now filled both my tags in less than a week! To top it off, I had finally gotten a buck, not a very big one, mind you, but a buck nonetheless. I was overjoyed!

The curse was finally broken! Over the next few seasons I became more selective about the quality of deer I would harvest, not for selfish motives, but to actively practice herd management. I decided I wouldn't take a buck unless he was awfully big, and I'd only harvest a lone yearling doe or a big mature one who didn't have any youngsters with her. As a result I passed up many opportunities to fill more tags. I passed up lots of young, immature bucks and quite a few does who were still nurturing their young. I took a few does during those more thoughtful seasons, but I was still looking for a big buck.

Thankfully, as a result of having learned to be gracious and satisfied with whatever happened in the woods, I never caught the trophy-hunting fever as it applies to whitetails. But that's not to say I wasn't actively pursuing them. At the beginning of one particular season I decided to take a day and do nothing but scout every inch of the property I was hunting on. I had become quite content with the success I was having in my favorite stand locations, but I had a hunch that there just might be some real undiscovered hot spots out there.

I traveled for what seemed like miles alongside a barbed-wire fence that led me through some rough terrain. As I began a slow descent down into a long and deep valley, I noticed several huge rubs and dozens of scrapes scattered throughout the area. I quickly picked up on the fact that this was a primary funnel area with lots of deer traveling through, including what appeared to be some good bucks. As I excitedly moved along, I came across a slightly chewed up shed antler that belonged to a big eight pointer. That was it! I knew this was the spot!

I quickly set up a stand and let it sit for a few weeks so the deer would get used to it. And sure enough, over the next few weeks I saw lots of deer from that stand, including some decent bucks, one of which I was very tempted to take, but thankfully held off. The next opportunity I had to hunt that stand was the afternoon of November 6. It was the first significantly cold day of the season. In fact, that was the evening of the first frost. I almost didn't hunt that day, but the call of the wild was in the air! I could feel it! I knew that something was going to happen. I had no choice but to go hunting.

It was a cold, biting afternoon, but I warmed up quickly as a result of the long walk to my new stand location. I climbed up and strapped myself in, knowing that something was fixin' to happen. Not long after I settled in, I heard an explosive commotion in the tree line behind me. I looked over my shoulder and saw two does bolting down the hill. Their white tails bobbed up and down as they raced off in a flash though the thick cedar trees and across the creek bed. Something had obviously spooked them, but what?

About twenty minutes later I heard some more loud crashing noises from behind me. I again slowly peeked around the other side of my tree to have a look. Moving very cautiously along the tree line was a huge deer. It was about seventy-five yards away, and I couldn't yet make out if it was a buck or a doe, but it was big. As the hulking figure continued to move closer, I soon confirmed that it was a buck, a big buck! Every year I have at least one encounter with a big buck, but this time he was moving in my general direction.

When he got to about forty-five yards away, he stopped as if deciding which way to go. Fearing that he'd go in the other direction, I knew I had to make a move. I carefully raised my deer call and made a few estrus doe bleats followed by some low buck grunts. He heard it, and it filled him with a jealous rage! He quickly snapped his head to attention. He proceeded to angrily make a scrape and violently thrash his antlers in a tree as if preparing for war! He laid back his ears, bristled up his coat, and aggressively marched in the direction of what he thought was an intruder. I silently screamed to myself, "Holy smokes, he's coming my way!" He was heading directly to my tree!

Being that my stand was a good twenty feet up in the tree, he had no idea I was there as I quickly and quietly drew back my bow in one smooth motion. When he got to about seventeen yards, I let out a semi-loud, man-made grunt to stop him. Sure enough, he stopped dead in his tracks and looked around for the source of the noise. My concentration could have burned a hole through him, but my arrow did the job instead. Being that I was so high up, and that I wanted to drop him as fast as possible, I sent the arrow right through his spinal column. It sounded like a two-by-four snapping in half as the arrow found its mark and the deer dropped within just a few yards.

"Oh my God, I did it! Oh my God I did it! I can't believe it! Holy Sweet Lord Jesus, I did it! Thank you dear God! Thank you dear God! Woooo Hooooo!" I don't need to point out that I was beside myself with excitement. I joyfully trembled and shook so hard that I almost fell out of the tree. I fumbled around as fast as I could to put away my gear and lower all my stuff down. I practically slid down the tree like a fireman's pole and raced over to the mighty buck. I forced myself to slow down enough to check and make sure he was fully expired. After confirming that he would not be getting up and running off, or ramming those antlers though my chest, I curiously and ecstatically examined this beautiful beast of a deer. He was a fine specimen of a mature ten point Missouri buck. (That 10th point is a bit small, but hey, it's still big enough to hang a ring on, barely.)

After spending some quality time thanking God and savoring that sacred moment, I knew I'd better get to work fast. I grabbed the deer's antlers and attempted to start the victorious drag out of the woods, but I barely budged him as I pulled with all of my might. It was then I knew that I'd be in for a long evening! I freshened my grip, squatted low to the ground and again pulled with all I had! He slid a little, but not much. Frantic, and considering what to do, I first set my camera on a stump to get a few self portraits (literally) and then whipped out my razor-sharp field-dressing knives. I gutted and dressed out that deer in record time, but also sliced my hand open on the broadhead tipped arrow that was still protruding from the deer's spine. Luckily it wasn't too bad of a cut, so I cleaned it up and carried on.

With the buck now being quite a few pounds lighter as a result of the emergency weight-loss program I administered to it,

I was able to drag him a little easier, but not much. My mind raced as I asked myself in a panic, "How in the world am I going to get this thing out of here? How am I possibly going to get this sucker to the check station in time? What if I have to leave it here overnight? Will coyotes eat it up? What if someone else comes along and tampers with him?" In a wild fit of hysteria I hooked up the other end of my safety harness to the buck's antlers, and pulled like an ox! With enough adrenalin rushing through my system to kill a lowland gorilla, I pulled that 200-pound deer several hundred yards in one mad rush, all uphill! (I'm not kidding!)

Finally collapsing, on the verge of a heart attack and absolutely physically exhausted, I knew I had to calm down and deal with the situation rationally. I reassured myself that, first of all, there was no way I was going to get him out of there that evening. Second, with the coming frost the meat would be fine; in fact, it would be beneficial to let him hang for a while. Third, I could hang him high in a tree to keep the coyotes away. Fourth, I could come back the next morning with some help to drag him out. And finally, I had until the next day to legally check him in. With that, I went and got the landowner to help me hang him from a tree for the night. I came back in the next morning with a buddy and pulled him out the rest of the way. I still can't believe I got that buck as far as I did on my own. It was difficult to pull that dude out of there even with two people!

When it was all said and done, the meat finally made it to the grill and the head now graces my wall. Every time I look at that deer I simply cannot believe that I got him. I continue to thank the Lord every time I admire that buck's tall, beautiful, perfectly symmetrical antlers. I'll never forget the elation and indescribable joy of that evening.

I hunted the rest of that season, in search of a fall turkey or two, but mostly I just wanted to be out there, I had to be out there. I spent the time in the stand just thinking, praying, and reflecting on all sorts of things. One of the things I kept asking myself was, "How come things have changed for the better so drastically over the last few seasons? Was it luck? Was it coincidence? Was it a matter of all that preseason work and study paying off?" I concluded that it was a combination of all those factors. All that study and preseason scouting led me to hunt in the right places. Many of the new techniques and tactics I put into practice definitely worked in getting the deer in close for a shot. And yes, it did seem to be coincidence that the deer were using those particular travel patterns, those particular seasons, on those particular days and times that I just happened to be in the stand.

Most of all, my renewed attitude made a huge difference. I found that when I was not dead set on things working out exactly like I wanted, as I had been in the past, when I was able to just let go and enjoy myself no matter what happened, things in turn did start to happen. I read somewhere that the Native Americans believed that the animals they hunted could sense their ego. It was believed that if one went into the woods with the attitude of, "I'm going to get a deer! I'm going to get a deer! I'm going to get a deer no matter what!" then the deer would pick up on that overdriven arrogant consciousness and would be spooked by it. On the other hand, if one went into the woods in a state of true spiritual/mental peace and harmony and was focused, but not worked up into a crazed frenzy, then the deer would be much more at ease.

I know I'm not by any means the first to say it, but there really seems to be something to that. Every time in the past that I would have a deer come by my stand while I was in that "I'm going to get you no matter what" mind-set, they always got spooked. It was as if they could feel my eyes on them and sense my overbearing mental (and physical) presence. They knew something was wrong. Even if I had no intention of harvesting them, they still got very wary. On the other hand, once I did away with that selfish, greedy attitude and focused on just being at ease, deer seemed to start coming out of the woodwork. I also found that I was more able to control and harness that adrenalin rush and use it to my advantage instead of letting it totally unravel me.

I noticed that the same phenomenon would occur when I went fishing as well. When I kept myself in a gracious, pleasant state of mind, body, and soul, fish just seemed to automatically attach themselves to the end of my line. Was it because they sensed that I was no immediate threat to them? Was it because I wasn't giving off some kind of greedy vibe? Was it because I became a part of the natural world instead of its dominating conqueror? Who knows? But something certainly changed for the better.

I firmly believe that having all that newfound success was ultimately the direct result of trusting in God and being thankful no matter what happened. Success cannot be forced with anything in life. It is a process of learning how to do the labor, of actually doing the labor, and then enjoying the fruit of that labor. Dishonesty and greed spoil the fruit, and overbearing expectations sour it.

Expectations play a big role in our lives. Unmet, unrealistic, or misguided expectations are the root of almost every sinful inclination known to man. A wise old monk once explained to me that at the heart of every struggle we have in life and at the heart of every sin we commit, there is at the very root of it an unfulfilled expectation. We have specific expectations regarding how certain things in our lives should work out. And when they don't work out according to those expectations, we get angry, sad, disappointed, etc. We then usually seek to express those reactionary feelings, which are perfectly healthy and normal in and of themselves, in ways that are not so healthy and normal. We get angry about something, so we lash out at others or hold it in and self-destruct.

We get sad about something, so we give up and drown ourselves in self-pity and lose all motivation. We get disappointed with something or someone, so we flush the whole works down the great toilet of life.

Almost all of those expectations or desires that we have are at the very core good ones. But when we fail to meet those expectations and fulfill those desires in holy and healthy ways, we then fulfill them in unhealthy and unholy ways — we sin. People desperately try to fill those voids with all sorts of bad stuff: with excesses of all kinds, with too much food, drink, drugs, stimulants, pornography, sexual sins, and so on. People who cannot deal with a particular family member or situation at home often become workaholics and engage in all sorts of avoidance behaviors. Those who have great difficulty with someone at work or school may find themselves acting out in passive-aggressive ways and doing all sorts of mean little things to get back at that person instead of having an open and honest confrontation or discussion about it. No matter what the situation, if it's not being dealt with in a good way, then it will most certainly be dealt with in a bad way, which only perpetuates the problem.

Surrendering those things to God is the only solution. To "surrender" does not mean to give up and stop trying; it means to stop beating ourselves to death and to trust that God will work with us and guide us to a holy solution. Most importantly, we have to realize that God is not going to come down and magically solve all of our problems for us. He will give us the grace, the strength, the wisdom and the courage to do what needs to be done, but we still have to put forth the effort and actually do it. There is no easy way out. But keep in mind that the most difficult things in life are also the most freeing. True freedom is not simply being able to do whatever the heck we want, when we want, and how we want. It's not about taking the easy way out.

True freedom is having the actual ability to choose what is good and reject what is bad, having the will to carry out that decision, and to responsibly deal with the outcome.

Allow me to explain. Some time ago, I came across a talk show in which the host was interviewing people about the significant cultural changes that occurred in the 1970s. They covered all the bases. They talked about the rampant drug use, the tremendous rise in promiscuous sexual activity, and the celebration of the homosexual lifestyle that began to emerge. They discussed people breaking away from the "captivity" of traditional religious beliefs and embracing the newfound "freedom" to do things like have an abortion and the easier access to things like artificial contraception. For a large number of people, true hedonism became the religion of the time.

Toward the end of the show, they discussed how so many died from drug overdoses and how sexually transmitted diseases and AIDS became a real threat and began to claim a significant number of lives. They pointed out that many ended up with all kinds of addictions that would haunt them for the rest of their lives. Many people didn't realize until later (and many still don't realize) how profoundly destructive, unhealthy, and dehumanizing abortion and artificial contraception could be.

Yet with all the extremely negative trends and consequences that this era produced, which have only grown worse over time, the way this show summed it all up was that it was one of the most liberating times in America. "People finally learned to be free," was the conclusion. When I heard this, I became enraged by the absurdity of such a statement.

Are the chains of addiction freedom? Is not being able to control one's passions freedom? Is weakening oneself to the point of no longer having any power of the will liberating? All of us have willpower, but willpower must be exercised in order to grow strong and be of any use. How is dying a miserable death as a result of a life of debauchery being free? Is a lifestyle in which physical intimacy and "love" are expressed by means of sodomy really all that natural, healthy, and holy? The statistics speak for themselves. How is ending the life of an unborn child or treating the sacredness of one's fertility like a disease an act of freedom?

I imagine the devil is having a good laugh at our expense. He's done a great job of distorting the truth regarding freedom. The Christian definition of freedom is that it is the ability to choose what is good, to *not* be chained to sin, to be able to say no and reject things that destroy us physically, emotionally, and spiritually. It's the ability to actively and aggressively reject what is evil and embrace what is good. Freedom is that which strengthens our virtue and draws us nearer to God and one another.

It's the lack of freedom that shuts the door in God's face, which separates us from him and each other, that promotes and generates destruction, death and disease, and that rejects any sense of commitment and responsibility. Being able to sin is not freedom; it's captivity. And that captivity is ultimately the punishment for sin, which we bring upon ourselves. Being able to commit sin is not a great privilege; it's the result of miserably failing in the midst of temptation because we didn't have the grace of God to keep us strong.

All of us by means of our human nature are subject to fall into sin, and true freedom is the ability to say no to that temptation. That's true freedom of choice. The more we embrace what is good, what is holy, and what is truly of God, the freer we become, because we are then more able to avoid that which separates us from him.

I heard the analogy once that sin is like an addictive substance for the soul. The more of it that gets in our system, the harder it becomes to break away from it. And as time goes on, it becomes increasingly more difficult to break away from it. We become slaves to it. We get so used to falling flat on our faces and failing time and time again that we lose all hope for success. We get so accustomed to the misery and bitterness of defeat that we completely lose touch with how joyful and how great it is to be victorious.

We can even train ourselves to fail. When, by the grace of God, something finally goes right in our lives and we've been able to finally break the chains of sin that have held us captive for so long, we can actually convince ourselves (with the help of the devil) that it won't last, that it's just been a lucky coincidence. We can become so uncomfortable with success that we are willing to plunge ourselves back into a life of sin. We willingly lock ourselves back up in prison because it's been the only life we've known for so long.

Knowing that we can succeed is an unbelievably empowering realization. It fills us with confidence and hope. And the more we get used to succeeding, the more potent that confidence and hope become. It begins to overflow into all areas of our lives. We come to acknowledge the fact that if we can overcome difficulties, rise to the challenge, put in the work, and see the fruits of our labor in one area of our lives, then we very well can do it in others.

There is, however, the attractive temptation to think that all of our success has been completely of our own doing and that we are solely responsible for the great things we've suddenly been able to accomplish. We have to always be humble enough to recognize that the success we experience is ultimately rooted in God. Whether we realize it or not, *God is the source of all that is good*. He is at the very core of the motivation, the hard work, and the discipline that leads to our success. He is the one who empowers us with his grace to experience the sweetness of success. And when we fully realize that, oh how sweet it is!

CHAPTER 14

Talking Turkey

GOOBBLEEABLAABLABLA! Goobbleee-Goobblobboolobbllee-ablaabla! There is nothing quite like hearing the thunderous spine-tingling sound of a big tom turkey gobbling at first light on a magical spring morning. Igor Stravinsky could have summed up his musical masterpiece *The Rite of Spring* with just one big long gobble. It's a wonderful sound that conjures all sorts of feeling and images. Whenever I hear that raspy gobble I think of fresh, green, dew-covered grass emerging from the remains of the long since decayed forest floor. I think of tall sunflowers displaying their happy faces to all the passers-by. That crazy gobbling fills me with an exuberant excitement and makes me think of cool mornings spent journeying to a lofty ridge top and awaiting the joyous sounds of a choir of gobbling toms at first light. I think of warm afternoons spent recuperating from the early morning fatigue and admiring the new life bursting forth all around me.

There is nothing quite as stunning as a tom turkey in full strut. Those vibrant dark colors and spectacular fanned-out tail feathers are highlighted only by his patriotic red, white, and blue head. His handsome symmetry is completed by his proud, puffed-up, tasseled chest. To watch a strutting tom turkey model his wears is the natural world's equivalence to being on a fashion show runway. It's no wonder that the turkey was almost chosen to be our national bird.

But make no mistake my friend, the wild turkey is a crafty one! Oh, so crafty! Those beady little eyes are almost impossible to elude. A stealthy tiptoeing turkey can creep by even the most well-tuned hearing aid. If it wasn't for the turkey's rich, dark feathers and curious vocals, they'd be virtually invisible. Many veteran turkey hunters say that those wily birds can see the blink of a man's eye from a hundred yards. And from my experience thus far, I believe they are right.

As of this writing, and after almost a decade of hunting turkeys, I still have not bagged a bird. Can you believe that!? Every single season that I've hunted I've had incredible, action-packed, heart-pounding encounters with those feathered fiends, but I always come home birdless. I do quite well with the actual hunting part, but I just have not been able to close the deal. Every time I go turkey hunting the same thing happens: I locate the birds, I get a big ol' tom fired up and gobbling like crazy, he comes into my calling like clockwork, and then either stays just out of range, gets spooked and takes off, comes in behind me, or stays behind an obstacle of some kind.

I've tried everything from using various decoy setups, hunting from a blind, using all sorts of different calling strategies, and hunting with someone else doing the calling, and still I can't get the job done. I'm convinced that I have some kind of horrible voodoo turkey hex on me. Perhaps I've consumed a cursed turkey at a thanksgiving dinner from years past. Maybe I've contacted some kind of turkey repelling juju from an ancient pagan burial ground that I might have accidentally stumbled upon. I just can't explain it. As much as those sneaky devils initially react to my calling, as much as they probably wish it were a lovely, lonely hen they were conversing with, they just seem to know its me and are able to muster enough gumption to pull themselves away and break free of my turkey-calling spell at the last possible moment. I must say, however, that all in all, I'm not too upset about my bad luck. I enjoy it so much and I always have such a great time in the turkey woods that it's just impossible to go home angry.

I absolutely love turkey hunting. It's really that simple. Perhaps it's the musician in me that enjoys the musical quality of calling and interacting with the birds. Maybe it's the opportunity to get out into the woods again long after deer season is over. It could be that the lush green grass, the gentle rain showers and the explosion of spring colors are what lure me into the turkey timber. I can't quite narrow it down to one thing, but there is something about the turkey-hunting experience that just plain makes me happy. It brings a hearty smile to my face and fills my soul with glee!

I've only had one experience of turkey hunting that was not fun. In fact, it turned into a life-threatening encounter with the raw rage of Mother Nature. Back in chapter four you may recall that I promised to share with you another epic tale of outdoor disaster. The experience of being stuck on that island on the Mississippi River with my good friend Jay was pretty darn rough, but escaping the fury of a flash flood (the worst one in 50 years) was also an ordeal I won't soon forget. That's what happened on one particular fateful hunting trip several years ago.

It started off being a beautiful May afternoon when Jay and I took off for a weekend of camping and turkey hunting. Final exams were over, school was out, and life couldn't get any better as we loaded up our vehicles and hit the highway. Good-time country tunes flowed out of my speakers and into the cool, rushing air as we rolled on down the line en route to our destination. The initial excitement of a trip like that is always contagious. It spreads over oneself like an oozing, itching case of poison ivy that just can't be contained. The smiles on our faces got bigger and wider as we practiced our turkey calls and checked out all our silly new hunting gadgets.

We finally made it to our spot, unpacked our stuff, set up camp, and began to engage in some heavy duty relaxing. We had a few hours to kill before we went out trying to locate birds for the evening, so we used the time just taking it easy. As evening came upon us and we stealthily searched the timber for roosting gobblers, there was an eerie calm in the woods and in the air. Something just didn't feel right.

As we gathered back at our campsite and watched the sun go down, we noticed a few sprinkles of rain coming out of the slightly overcast sky. We didn't give it much concern, being that we checked the forecast and learned that there was a slight chance of showers for that evening. But that was supposed to be it. Well, once again, that was not it. Not by a long shot!

Being that we were camping out in our own vehicles (Jay in his truck, me in my van) and not in a tent like our previous nightmarish endeavor, we figured that a little, or even a lot of evening precipitation couldn't do all that much harm. As I listened to the gentle pitter patter of raindrops on the roof of my van, I cozied up in my sleeping back and was fast asleep with visions of gobblers strutting in my head.

The gentle rain soon evolved into a torrential downpour, and that turned into a thunder and lightning storm like nothing I'd ever experienced, and that turned into a furious temper tantrum from a very angry Mother Nature. Before it was all over, tornadoes, hail, and an unimaginable natural violence was unleashed upon us. It was so bad that it was impossible to see anything or go anywhere in an attempt to escape the growing fury. For the first time in my life, I was truly fearful of the power of nature. We had no choice but to stay put and ride out the apocalyptic storm that was vulgarly displaying its power.

The lightning was striking all around us, seemingly charring the rain-soaked earth with a mad rage! The thunder was so loud that I thought my skull would split open from the crushing decibels! The wind rocked my van as if it were being blasted by a war-mongering tank whose mission was to obliterate everything in its path!

I stayed sprawled out on the floor of my van, gripping tight in order to keep from being swept away into oblivion. At some point, I heard a strange rhythmic pounding on the back of my van and what I thought was some kind of bizarre hollering sound. As I found out later, it was Jay trying to get my attention to get the heck out of there. It was still too dangerous to do or go anywhere, so we decided to wait until first light to make our move.

As we emerged into the still violent morning conditions from what could have been our mobile tombs, we noticed that the tiny trickle of a creek, which we intentionally parked way back from (several hundred yards), now looked like the Missouri River coming though the field and rising quick! The churning whitewater rapids of this preborn river of death were approaching us very fast and appeared to be gaining a maniacal force with every passing moment. The edge of the water was about twenty yards from where we were. We packed up our belongings and proceeded to evacuate the premises immediately!

Jay led the way in his 4x4 truck and I tried to follow close behind, but my ill-equipped little van could not stay on course through the swampy mud that used to be a gravel road. I went about fifty yards and got hopelessly stuck! After a few futile efforts to get out, I was quick to learn that my poor red van was stuck for good. I threw my stuff in Jay's truck and we still barely made it out, even with four-wheel drive. After getting out of the immediate area, we headed to higher and dryer ground. We made it up the top of a hill and stayed put until the grand finale of the storm finished its encore performance.

We heard on the radio that fifteen inches of rain fell overnight. Two people were dead, several were missing, lots of folks had to abandon their homes, and basically we were in the heart of an official disaster zone. As the rain continued to pour down, Jay and I sat in his truck in a state of complete shock, amazed at what we had again gotten ourselves into and thankful that we made it out alive. When I finally made it back home, the exhaustion of the whole ordeal set in and I collapsed and slept for the next twelve hours.

I was not able to get my van out of the muck until several days later when the waters subsided and things dried out a bit. Once again, what was supposed to be a few days of relaxing enjoyment turned into an introduction to hell! As you can most likely guess, no birds were bagged on that trip, either.

Though I've yet to delight in a wild turkey dinner, at least one that I've been responsible for, there is one experience in particular that I wouldn't trade for any amount of turkey-hunting success in the world. How often does one call in the exceptionally hyperalert wild turkey and have it walk up and almost literally sit on one's lap? That's exactly what happened to me on the opening day of the season a few years ago.

That spring there again had been lots of rain and it continued well into the turkey season. I was unable to get out and locate birds the evening before, so I decided that I'd head up to my favorite ridge top first thing in the morning before the sun came up and listen for where the gobblers were. As always, when the yellow ochre of the sun illuminated the moist emerald green sprouts of the new forest undergrowth and the world began to wake up, the gobbling started to echo throughout the valley. There was not as much gobbling as usual due to the pouring rain that continued to soak me to the bone and send a slight shiver though my body, but there were a couple of noisy birds who seemingly wanted to play.

I hunkered down, leaned back, and nestled into the almost form-fitting shape of my favorite oak tree. Camouflaged from head to toe with my shotgun readied, I began a calling sequence to see if I could get the birds interested in coming my way. After a fun but fruitless interaction with a rainy-day gobbler who was most likely on his way to a nice open field somewhere (as turkeys like to do when the rain comes), I decided to take a little snooze and relocate later in the morning. I've always liked the rain, and I was so cozy just snuggling up with that tree that I wanted to stay right there and enjoy the moment.

A half hour or so went by, and as I slowly opened my groggy eyes I saw a big hen turkey about fifty yards out. Female turkeys cannot be taken during the spring season in Missouri, but I thought I'd have some fun and try talking to her a bit. I had a diaphragm call in my mouth, which allowed me to remain totally still while calling, and so I began making some soft yelps and purring sounds to see how the bird would react. The big hen starting moving in my direction while answering back with some relaxed clucks and whimsical yelps. The closer she got, the quieter I called.

When she was about fifteen yards away I shut up completely to see what she'd do then. I'll never forget the shocked excitement and delirious unbelief that pulsated through my entire being as she carefully stepped right in my direction. She tiptoed to within inches of where I was sitting. She stopped, looked me up and down, and then almost stepped right in my lap! She backed off a little, and as we looked at each other, literally eyeball to eyeball, I realized that this has got to be about the rarest and coolest thing that has ever happened to me in the woods.

She stayed right at my side for about five minutes and continued to look around for the bird she was hearing. I could have easily reached out and touched her. She backed off a little more and hopped up on a fallen tree about five feet away from me. She began preening her feathers and then just sort of stood there for about ten minutes. I very carefully began to do some more calling and she again began to wander around looking for the mysterious, invisible companion she was hearing. After cautiously searching the immediate area once more, she finally gave up and wandered back down the ridge. Wow! That was so awesome! That was something I never thought I'd experience in a million years. The satisfaction of that phenomenally intimate experience with the wildest of wild birds was enough to erase all the disappointment of not actually getting a bird.

You just never know what's going to happen when you're in the woods. The excitement of that expected unexpectedness is what brings me (and countless others) back to the forest time and time again. If I were dead set on getting a bird and totally focused on that goal and that goal only, I probably never would have had that incredible experience. I probably would have given up turkey hunting long ago. One of the greatest keys to the true enjoyment that the outdoors offers and ultimately the key to success that does eventually come, is learning to surrender, to be satisfied with whatever happens, and to realize how much of a gift it is to simply be an active participant with the natural world. As discussed in a previous chapter, it's about learning to become a part of nature instead of being its careless, intruding dominator.

The same is true of life: You just never know what's going to happen. And if we are so focused on things happening exactly how we want, we end up missing out on so many other wonderful things that we never would have expected. In the realm of the spiritual, we call it "surrendering to the will of God." I addressed this subject a little in the previous chapter, but to go into more detail, we hear in Scripture that "No eye has seen, nor ear heard, nor the heart of man conceived, what God has prepared for those who love him" (1 Cor 2:9). God has things in store for us that are far beyond our wildest imagination. The blessings and gifts that God desires to give us are more than we could ever comprehend and are much more than we ever deserve. But so often we never even acknowledge or appreciate those gifts and blessings because of our greediness, our selfishness, and our inability to surrender to the will of God.

When we think of "surrendering," we often think in terms of giving up, of being defeated, of being forced into submission by an overbearing and highly superior adversary of some kind. This is not what surrendering to God is all about. Surrendering to the will of God is simply a matter of admitting that God knows us far better than we could ever know ourselves, that he has a plan and a purpose for us, and that he will give us what we need, though not necessarily what we always want. Surrendering to the will of God is simply allowing God to take control of our lives, to guide us along the right path; it is to trust and to believe that he is with us always and that he will help us through those difficult times. It's accepting the fact that he loves us and that he wishes us to share in that love both on earth and in heaven.

When we ask, "What is God's will for me?", we often think in terms of deciphering some detailed work order, of somehow figuring out an elaborate plan, or of unraveling a precariously confusing divine mystery of some sort that God has placed before us. We can easily drive ourselves to the brink of madness as we hold on to the false notion that we must meticulously and perfectly figure out this cosmic puzzle that God has given us before we can truly begin to live our lives in accordance with God's will. Well, my friend, you'll be glad to know that's it's much easier than that!

After years of intense soul-searching, I finally discovered God's will while coming home from my brother's wedding in Pittsburgh. The wedding was a joyful event and a beautiful celebration, as all weddings are, but the long 15-hour ride back home was agonizing. It seemed to take forever. The miles slowly dragged on. I was traveling with my parents and everybody was tired and worn out and just seemed to be lost in their own thoughts. That was the only trip to this day that I can distinctly remember exactly what I was thinking about during that arduous journey home.

At the time, I was in my second year of seminary and I was struggling tremendously with my vocation. I didn't know if I was on the right path. I was worried that perhaps I was making a terrible mistake. I was consumed with thoughts of other things that I could possibly be doing with my life, such as getting married and starting a family like my brother had just done.

As we drove on, while still consumed with worries and confusion, I began to pray. I pleaded with the Lord to show me the way. I begged him for a sign to let me know that I was doing his will and that I was on the right track. I asked God over and over again very aggressively, "What do you want me to do? What am I to do with my life? What is your plan for me? How am I to serve you?" I wanted specific answers. I demanded specific answers. This prayerful interrogation of God went on for several hours. And the answers didn't seem to come. I began to get very aggravated and angry, demanding his guidance.

I kept repeating over and over again, "What do you want me to do?" And then something happened. Suddenly, my dad, who almost never listens to the radio while driving, did something I'd very rarely seen him do; he actually turned on the radio. And just as I was asking that question, "What do you want me to do?" the voice of a radio preacher, accompanied by static, came through the speakers and exclaimed, "You've got to love!" Right after he said that, the static completely drowned him out, we lost the signal, and my dad turned the radio off.

I have no doubt in my mind that the voice coming through that radio was the voice of the Holy Spirit. And that obvious, simple message hit me like a sledgehammer. At that point in my life I hadn't really thought about love in a long time. I was too busy asking God questions and wasn't listening for answers. From that moment on, I began to really focus on what it means to love; to love God, to love others, to live out that self-sacrificing love of Christ.

Jesus tells us, "The Holy Spirit, whom the Father will send in my name, he will teach you all things, and bring to your remembrance all that I have said to you" (Jn 14:26). How true this is. As I've already pointed out several times throughout this book (once more can't hurt), the Holy Spirit is at work all the time. He speaks to us, guides us, and inspires us every day. But so often we get so caught up in the questions that we fail to hear the answers. And usually the answers to our heart-wrenching, soul-churning questions are unbelievably simple. They're so simple that when we finally do realize what the answer is, we can feel like a complete fool. There was a time in all of our lives when we didn't know what one plus one equaled. And we might have screamed and pouted and begged our teacher or parents to tell us the answer. But most likely they didn't just hand over the answer; they patiently helped us to learn it.

What is God's will for you and me and everybody else? It is to love God, to love one another, and to avoid the things that will destroy that love. Is it God's will that you become a doctor, live in Timbuktu, have three kids, drive a red truck, and eat chicken tonight and pork chops tomorrow? If that will enable you to love God, love others, and avoid sin to the best of your ability, then yes. The specifics are not that important for us to figure out. God will not *make* us do anything. He loves and respects us enough to give us the freedom to choose our own path, even if it makes us miserable. If we truly strive to seek his love and avoid sin as our top priority, then the specifics will come. Doors will open and other doors will shut. But once those doors are shut, it's important to leave them shut. One can't move forward while still looking back.

No matter what the specifics of God's will may be for us, we can be assured of one thing: that nobody gets a free and easy ride. No matter what road we take, we will face struggles and challenges; we will face heartaches and difficulties of all kinds. Of course, there will be lots of good times, joy, and happiness as well, but things will not always work out as we hoped for and planned. There will be many sacrifices to be made along the way.

No matter what we've done, could have done, or will ever do in the course of our lives, the reality is that nothing will be perfect. We will not achieve a state of perpetual happiness while here on earth. *No-thing* and *no-one* can *make* us happy. No amount of antidepressants, psychotherapy, entertainment, food, drink, hobbies, sex, drugs, rock-n-roll, or anything else can *make* us happy. The ultimate truth is that not even God can *make* us happy. We have to be willing to be happy. We have to allow ourselves to be happy. We have to truly want to be happy.

Everybody in every walk of life, of every social status, and of every time and place experiences emptiness, loneliness, heartache, pain, frustration, loss, doubt, and despair. We all have times that we question the meaning of our lives, the purpose of our existence, and the truth of our reality. Everybody has those moments when they wish they were someone else, that they had a different life, lived in a different place, had a different job, a different family, a different set of looks, and different talents. And we can change our job, change our lifestyle, and change our looks. We can live in a different town, in a different place, and get to know different people and do different things. We can pretend we're someone else and betray the very nature of who God intended us to be. The grass will always look greener on the other side and we will always wonder, "What if . . . ?"

Yes indeed, if you are a human being living on planet earth, you will be in for a rough ride no matter what path you choose. But there are road signs along the way to assure us that we are on the right path, and that we are doing the will of God. As the spiritual greats of centuries ago have pointed out, the sure sign that we are doing God's will is a lasting sense of peace in the midst of whatever storms may come our way.

To use myself as an example, sometimes being a priest really stinks! There are times that I intensely question my vocational decision and even painfully regret it. When things are going extremely bad and it seems like everything I'm doing is a complete waste of time, I find myself taking a good look at those doors that have been long shut. The realization that I could have done lots of other things with my life, things that might have been more enjoyable and that I might have been much better at, hits me hard. There is always that temptation to start fantasizing about leaving it all behind and starting over somewhere, somehow, someway.

But then the reality hits me. Yes, there are many other things in life that I could be doing, and there are certainly other paths that I could have chosen, that may have been more satisfying and enjoyable. But *this* is the path that *I* have *freely* chosen. This is the path that I firmly believe God has invited and called me to travel. I could have said no, and that would have been fine. But despite all the struggles and frustration, there is a peace in my soul (though sometimes it's hard to find it) that tells me that this is God's will for me, that this is where I belong, that this is the way, the how, and the where. This path is what is leading me (and hopefully others) to the "way, the truth, and the life." I know deep down that if I were doing something else with my life, that lasting peace would not be there.

That sense of peace is the direct result of a prayerful and loving commitment to God's will. No matter what path one may choose, one has to make a serious and lasting commitment to it in order for that way of life to produce fruit. Without that commitment to what we have freely chosen and what God has called us to, everything crumbles like the house the foolish man built on sand (see Mt 7:26-27). We must firmly commit and regularly recommit ourselves to the people, the work, and the responsibilities that have come with the vocation in life that we have been called to and that we have freely chosen. The rock solid foundation that we are to build our lives upon is our relationship with God. Without God to keep us strong when those storms of life come our way, we then begin to seek shelter in places and in ways that only contribute to our personal and spiritual destruction.

We've already seen that a relationship with God takes real commitment. But let me remind the reader again that we have to *make* the time daily to spend with him in prayer, even if it's just a few minutes. We have to *make* the effort to live out our faith to the fullest, especially when doing so might be very challenging and extremely uncomfortable. But on the simplest and most important level, the foundation of that relationship with God and the very core of who we are as Christians is found in what we do on Sunday morning in church.

For Catholics, it is found at Sunday Mass. Everything else we do flows from that fountain of grace. Every Sunday of the year is a continuation of the Easter celebration. At every Mass on every Sunday we celebrate the passion, death, and resurrection of Christ. And it is at every Mass that Christ continues to bestow upon us his transforming and empowering grace (whether we realize it or not). Going to church is not just something we do to kill time on a Sunday morning or because it's nice to do once in a while. Our weekly participation is our commitment and response to Jesus' *command* to "Do this in remembrance of me"

(Lk 22:19). It is also our response to the *command* of God the Father to keep holy the Sabbath day (see Ex 20:8).

As a priest, I'm always amazed at how many Christians (not just Catholics) don't think twice about missing church because of a sporting event or some other activity that may pop up on a Sunday morning. I'm amazed at how many folks miss church simply because they didn't feel like going or thought it would be too boring, so they decided to sleep in or go shopping instead. I'm amazed at how many can't make a commitment of one hour a week to say thank you — to say thank you to God for the gifts of our lives, our families and friends, and the countless blessings God has given us that we so often take for granted. Most of all, I can't believe how many don't take or make the time on a Sunday morning to say thank you to Jesus for shedding his blood, suffering, and dying a humiliating death on the cross so that we might have eternal salvation. It's amazing how quickly we forget about that sacrifice Jesus made for us and what it means.

Imagine if someone saved your life in a very dramatic manner. Imagine that you were doomed to suffer unbelievable horrors, and that your complete and total ruination was at hand. Imagine your worst fear multiplied a million times. Imagine that it is very real, and that it is coming for you like a vulture to a carcass. Let that imagined reality sink in for a moment. Now imagine that someone came along and saved you from that imminent, hopeless fate in the most heroic manner possible. Not only that, but in turn underwent that horror themselves as an act of love for you. Wouldn't you do anything and everything possible to show that person a monumental degree of gratitude? Wouldn't the selfless actions of that person dramatically change your life? Wouldn't you spend at least some part of every day of your life thinking about and thanking that person for saving your life? Couldn't you give at least one hour a week to honor that person? It's hopefully quite obvious what I'm getting at here. Think about it.

CHAPTER 15

Turkey Temptation

OPENING DAY OF YET ANOTHER spring turkey season was just a few weeks away. As I began to rummage though my box of hunting doodads and knick-knacks in search of my favorite turkey calls and gadgets, I began to feel the glorious excitement of that impending first day of the season. *Goodness gracious mercy sakes alive*, I couldn't wait to get out to the woods and once again hear that magical sound of a gobbling tom turkey! Just the slight thought of it gave me shivering goose bumps. However, I felt a bit unprepared as I hadn't even practiced my calling yet or even gotten my shotgun ready for action. Perhaps subconsciously I didn't even expect the possibility of bagging a bird. After all, don't forget I do have a fiendish turkey-hunting hex on me.

During the last week before the season started, I put things into high gear and organized my equipment, brushed up on my calling, did some target practice, and prayed to God that this season my luck would change. I had a good feeling. I had a hunch that things would go much better this year. The more I entertained my positive thoughts the more I downright convinced myself that this was going to be *the* season!

Sure enough, things got off to a great start. For the first time in several years it didn't pour down rain opening weekend. The birds were gobbling like crazy and all seemed right with the turkey universe. But wouldn't you know it, when it was all said and done, despite a marvelous opening day, no birds were bagged yet again. I didn't let it get me down, though. I knew that I'd be hunting my favorite farm for the rest of the season, and I still had a great feeling that something big (hopefully with feathers and a beard) was going to go down!

The next week rolled around and I eagerly headed out for round two. Once again things were looking good. There still had been little rainfall, which made crossing the creek that divided me from turkey-hunting heaven a piece of cake. I merrily skipped and hopped (in a manly way) across the big creek rocks to the other side. I then stood at the base of the massive hill, preparing to make my annual trek way up to my favorite ridge-top turkey-listening post. But then I stopped and thought for a moment. As I reflected on things, I called to mind the fact that every year I hear lots of turkeys from up there, but they are always way down below me, possibly roosting by the creek on the other side of the property. With that in mind, I decided to change my tactics.

I slowly eased along the side of the hill and carefully made my descent down to the area where I thought the turkeys would most likely sound off. As always, nothing responded to my locator calls (and I tried them all), so I decided to position myself slightly uphill from the creek-bottom area that connects a field to the thick (and I mean thick) woods. Sure as heck, a little before full sunup, the birds started sounding off like crazy! There was gobbling all around me, and close! I heard seven different birds all within easy calling range. By golly, I was right. Those birds were hanging out way down there, which was kind of strange being that turkey seem to usually roost somewhat uphill when they can.

When there was enough light to see what was going on around me and possibly shoot a bird, I began to do a series of calling. Three gobblers who sounded very close responded back without hesitation. I called back and forth with them for a while, but eventually some eager hens cut them off at the pass as they headed in my direction. All the gobbling tapered off for the time being, as I knew those birds were fairly preoccupied for the moment. I heard a few more gobbles off and on throughout the morning but nothing close again until about 7:45 A.M., when an earth-shattering gobble came from my left. My heart began to pound and my breathing grew fast and heavy as I hunkered down and got ready. I had some decoys in plain view, hoping to lure him in close, and so I called a bit more with some excited, passionate cutting sounds to get him fired up, and then I stopped. He roared back with a deafening, "GGOOOBBLLLEEEUUBBBBELLEELLLEEE!" He was coming in fast and hard!

As I stayed low and peered through the slight opening of my camouflaged face mask, I saw him come over the little hill and knew that the moment of truth had finally come after all these years! He was about forty-five yards away when he finally stepped into a bit of a clearing. His head was jerkily spinning around as he looked all over for the bird he thought he was hearing. Suddenly his eyes locked onto my decoys, and he got spooked. He turned around and started to go back in the other direction. It was a far shot to try and pull off, but I knew it was now or never, so I blasted him . . . BOOM!

As the shot echoed throughout the hillside, he hit the ground and rolled around. I got him! Or so I thought. But then he quickly hopped up and started trotting up the hill. I jumped up and took off after him as fast as I could. As he raced up the steep incline I stopped and got one more shot off at him but missed cold because he was still a ways off and moving fast. I was hot on his trail when he finally stopped and settled in next to a brush pile. I carefully watched him for a while, figuring he was soon to breathe his last. He just sat there with his head up looking around. I very slowly, step-by-inching-step, stalked up to within twenty-five yards of him. I then ever so cautiously raised my shotgun, put the bead right on his head, made good and sure my front and back sights were perfectly aligned and then slowly pulled the trigger. As the trigger eased back and came to a stop, all I heard was a "click." In shock and disbelief, I quickly tried to cycle another round, but then noticed that my gun was empty! Somehow, in all the excitement, I cycled my last live shell out of the gun and now had no ammo! I always make it a point to carry extra shells with me, but for some fateful reason I didn't that day. In fact, I remember saying to myself that morning as I was about to load my pockets full of ammo, "How many shells is it going to take to kill a bird? I won't need more than three." Wrong again, Joey ol' boy!

As I held my empty shotgun in my trembling hands and watched the bird of my dreams give me the evil eye from the protective confines of a large brush pile, I began to desperately try and come up with an idea to get that sucker! If I had had a spear, I could have stuck him with it. If I had had a big rock, I could have chucked it at him. If I had had a rope, I could have lassoed him. If I had had a huge knife or hatchet, I could have flung it at him, but none of those things were handy at the moment. All I had were my two hands (and a delicious cheese sandwich on whole wheat bread — hmmm, maybe I could have coaxed him out with that.) I realized that my only chance was to tackle him and ring his neck like a chicken!

I slowly eased forward, right up to him, almost in pouncing range. He hunkered down and still didn't move. I figured he was either badly hurt, shell shocked, or realized he didn't have much of anywhere to go. As I was almost ready to make my desperate pounce, I realized I would have to get around to the other side of him to get a good tackle. As I made my move he finally bolted! I chased him back down the hill and all around the densely thick woods. It was like a scene from a hillbilly comedy movie with some overzealous farmer, liquored up on moonshine, trying to catch a rooster. After several minutes of chasing that big gobbler through the woods, I finally cornered him up against a barbed wire fence. He had a look on his face like, "Oh boy, now what?"

I again got to within almost tackling distance, and then he crouched down, crawled under the fence, and raced down the hill toward the creek. Without a second thought, and after years of giving up my high-jumping career, I leaped over the fence and took off after him. He stopped again as if to catch his breath, as I tried to catch mine. We then got into a pickle that would no doubt please any major league baseball fan. I'd move right, he'd go left. I'd lunge forward, he'd dash backwards. Round and round we went. He still wasn't flying, so I figured that he was indeed either hurt, dazed and confused, or just realized that there was no place to fly to yet. After a bit of a standstill, he suddenly ran right at me. When he was almost within tackling range again, he took a hard left to the creek. At this point, I had to literally slap myself in the face to see if I was dreaming. "This just can't be happening," I thought. This is the most unbelievable thing that I could have ever possibly imagined!

In one last desperate attempt, I threw my (unloaded, of course) shotgun at the bird as he darted by me. He ducked and kept going. He finally made his way to the water's edge, looked back at me, jumped up and flew across the creek, across the field, and then kept on going until he was back in the woods on a different farm and out of my life forever! The thought of wounding that bird really bothered me, but he didn't seem to be too badly hurt once he got his wits back. I think (and hope) that I just knocked him silly.

My heart sank with disbelief as I watched that big bird fly away. All I had to remember him by was a feather he left behind in all the commotion. I just stood there for a while, still not believing what went down. Crazy stuff like that happens to me every year, but I never in my wildest dreams could have conjured an experience like that. For the rest of the week I couldn't help but find myself thinking about that bird and other possible scenarios of what I could have done in that desperate situation. I even entertained thoughts of illegal tactics that I could have possibly employed. I consider myself to be a very ethical hunter, abiding religiously by all the rules of the game. I would never actually attempt anything illegal when it comes to hunting and fishing, but isn't it strange how such tempting thoughts come when we find ourselves in moments of weakness, desperation, or despair?

Temptation comes to all of us in different ways and at different times. No one is free from the power of temptation, and all of us crumble under its weighty influence from time to time. When we hear the word "temptation" we usually think of it as something that draws us into sin. For someone who's given up smoking, a cigarette ad in a magazine picturing people having a great time while joyfully smoking themselves into oblivion will no doubt be a huge temptation. For someone who is trying to lose weight or maybe lower his or her cholesterol, passing up a big, greasy bacon cheeseburger may seem like an impossible task. For a turkey hunter trying to bag his first bird after years of failure, mowing it down with an AK-47 might seem like a good idea! No matter what it is we struggle with in life, there are loads of temptations out there.

A significant element of our present culture is that even if we make every effort to avoid the temptations that lead us into sin, those temptations will come looking for us, through things like the Internet, TV, radio, advertisements, and so on.

We often hear that the devil is the source of all temptation and evil. Scripture describes the devil as "a roaring lion, seeking someone to devour" (1 Pet 5:8). That's a perfect description. Just as God is the ultimate source of all that is good, there is also an ultimate source of all that is evil — the devil. Just as the grace of God can flow in us and through us and positively effect ourselves and others, so, too, evil can flow in us and through us and negatively affect ourselves and others, if we allow it. The devil stops at nothing regarding finding ways to lead us into sin. He aggressively seeks to destroy us and our relationship with God and one another. And, of course, his greatest trick is to make us believe he doesn't exist at all, that there is nothing to be on guard against.

The actual, original meaning of the word "temptation" is not so much about being coerced into doing something bad. The original meaning of the word "tempt" means to be tested. We see this throughout the Bible. The obedience of Adam and Eve was tested, and they failed to pass that test. In Scripture, we hear of different people being subjected to some very intense testing, and some, like Adam and Eve, failed the test, while others, like Abraham, who almost ended up sacrificing his son Isaac, passed the test. Jesus, the Son of God, was tested in the desert for forty days. Nobody is temptation-proof!

The experience of passing a test is what ultimately makes one stronger and thus more able to do great things for God, for others, and for oneself. When we were tested in school, it was to see if we had reached a certain level of accomplishment so we could then move on to bigger and better things. If we weren't able to pass that test, then trying to move on to those bigger and better things would likely have been a disaster, or at least extremely difficult.

If a runner can't run a few miles without being out of breath and being on the verge of collapse, then he or she will never be able to even attempt to run a marathon. The same thing applies to us spiritually. If we can't pass those small tests in life, we'll never be able to pass the big ones. And those big ones come to every-body sooner or later in different ways.

God allows us to be tempted, to be tested, because those are opportunities to grow stronger. But if we think that we can just grit our teeth and get through whatever comes our way on our own accord, we are sorely mistaken. It's only with the grace of God that we receive the strength and the courage to pass those tests. And, of course, we can be sure that those same tests will come our way again and again, just like those horrible algebra exams in high school. But with the grace of God, and a good measure of perseverance, those tests get easier and easier.

Out of all the temptations that are out there, out of all the sins that can really shatter lives, break relationships, and cause severe emotional, spiritual, and, at times, physical trauma, sexual sins would have to be at the top of the list. I always get a kick when people say about us priests, "You guys don't know what people have to deal with in life. You don't know what people go through in the real world." Lest one may forget, we priests hear confessions every week. I can say in full confidence that *no one* on the face of the earth knows more about the utter brokenness of humanity than we. People tell us things that they would never even dream of telling a psychologist or their most trusted friend or family mem-ber. We hear things that if spoken in the light of day could com-pletely destroy the life of that person. They come truly seeking an experience of God's forgiveness, and that is what they receive.

A priest can never, under penalty of excommunication, reveal the identity (which we usually don't know anyway) or the sins of a particular individual who has come to confession. With that said, keep in mind that what I'm going to be talking about here are generalizations.

Week after week, we priests hear from married people who have had an affair or have sought sexual gratification by means of visiting prostitutes, strip clubs, and so forth. We hear from young people who have been sexually active and are suffering the tremendous emotional pain that comes from unloving, uncaring sexual activity. We hear from people of all ages and all walks of life who are addicted to pornography and masturbation. We hear from those who are struggling with same-sex attractions and how their homosexual activity has confused and altered their sense of who they are as a human being. We hear from those who have sexually abused others or have been abused themselves. We hear from those caught up in very disturbing things like bestiality. We hear from people who have contracted various diseases or who have had abortions as the result of immoral sexual activity.

Any kind of sexual deviation or sin you could possibly imagine (please don't), you can bet your bottom dollar that we priests have heard it. Nothing is shocking to us. We are scandalized by nothing. All sin causes pain and misery, but sexual sins seem to have an enslaving characteristic uniquely their own. They ruin people's lives, their self-worth, their dignity, their trust, and their hope like nothing else.

I firmly believe that one of the top reasons people struggle so much with sexual sin is because of the amount of temptation that is out there these days. Not a day goes by that one is not blatantly assaulted with sexual imagery or content in one form or another. It is virtually everywhere. We see it on billboards while driving down the highway, on magazine covers at the grocery store checkout line, on radio and TV commercials, on junk e-mail and pop-ups. Even if you're trying to avoid it and steer clear of such material, it still stares you in the face at every corner. Our culture is infatuated with sex. Multi-million dollar companies thrive on selling their products with it. Pop stars become little less than pagan gods or goddesses because of it. Sitcoms laugh about it. "Art" celebrates it. Sex is the fuel that much of our culture thrives and lives on.

In a world with thousands of people dropping dead from AIDS and suffering from other sexually transmitted diseases, our culture thinks it's doing people a huge favor in saying things like, "Be safe, use a condom!" What a joke! Let me ask you this. If you are in a situation where having sexual intercourse is quite possibly going to give you a disease, bring a child into the world that you are not ready to take care of, or even kill you, do you really think you are doing the right thing? Are you willing to place a piece of rubber between you and your worst nightmare?

The Catholic Church gets a lot of flack these days over her teachings on sexual morality, especially those concerning things like artificial contraception and abortion. It's said that the majority of Catholics disagree with the Church's teaching on artificial contraception and many more disagree on other issues of sexual morality as well. As always, these harsh criticisms are mostly due to a severe lack of understanding on the part of the faithful and a severe lack of teaching on the part of the clergy. Many priests do not preach or teach on these issues for various reasons. Some fear the almost violent backlash that may occur when having the audacity to dare preach on some of these subjects. Some simply don't want to stir the pot and get their congregation riled up about such sensitive issues. Others don't themselves agree with the Church's stance on these things. Whatever the case may be, the word is not getting out and the faithful are remaining blinded and paralyzed by the lack of information and proper understanding of these issues.

The Catholic Church's teachings on sexuality are very powerful and very beautiful. Volumes have been written (but not necessarily read) on this topic over the years by popes, bishops, priests, and lay men and women. There is a lot of great stuff out there, but much of this material tends to be a bit too "heady" and theological for the average person sitting in the pew, who would need to take a semester's worth of classes just to understand the lingo of these documents. Thus, the relevance, potency, sincere beauty, and life-altering power of these teachings get lost in a catechetical, systematic, epistemological, ontological, metaphysical cloud of confusion.

For starters, the Church teaches that sexual intercourse is the ultimate expression of love between a man and a woman (more about that in a moment). "Love" is a very strong word. It's not just about really liking someone or being extremely attracted to someone. It's not just about a certain feeling one may identify as love. It's not just a particular frame of mind or affectionate disposition toward someone else. Love is about being totally committed to someone in good times and bad until nothing but death separates that relationship. As we've already seen, true love is a self-sacrificing love that is totally focused on the good of another.

True love is committed love. It outlasts the demeaning arguments that couples sometimes have. It goes beyond the change in physical appearance due to age, sickness, childbirth, and so on. It goes beyond the financial struggles and difficulties with family and work. It outlasts the many hardships and problems that will come throughout life. This is why the Church elevates marriage to a sacrament, to an experience in which one truly encounters (and needs) the very presence of God.

The Church views marriage as a sacred covenant and a committed partnership between man, woman, and God. When a couple receives the Sacrament of Marriage, they are promising a lifetime of commitment to their spouse and to God. They are promising to live out their faith in their married life together and to be active members of the Christian community, which means going to Church on days besides just Christmas and Easter or when they want to have their children baptized.

There is a great deal of confusion these days concerning the difference between a wedding and a marriage. As one of my seminary professors emphatically reminded us in class, a wedding, while very memorable and beautiful, lasts less than an hour. A marriage lasts a lifetime (or at least it's supposed to). With this being the case, one would think that there would be more emphasis on marriage instead of only focusing on the big day. In our secular society, this is obviously not the case. There are lots of TV shows, videos, books, and magazines about weddings, but there is hardly anything out there on marriage.

This unbalanced focus and the message it sends is the source of a lot of frustration, especially regarding Christian marriage. I (along with most priests) constantly deal with couples who are not going to church, who in all honesty want little or nothing to do with the church, who already live together and are sexually active, who do not support the church in any way, yet who want (and expect) to have a big traditional "church" wedding with all the bells and whistles.

Many of these couples are radically consumed with meticulously planning every possible last-minute detail of their big day, yet they have never once prayed together, gone to church together, or intimately discussed sensitive issues in their relationship that *will* rear their ugly heads sooner or later and possibly have a catastrophic impact on their marriage. I'm thoroughly convinced that if couples would spend half as much time truly preparing for marriage as they do intensely working on all the details of their wedding, we probably wouldn't have a fifty percent divorce rate in our country.

For the Christian, marriage is the sacred celebration of a sacred love. The most sacred, powerful, unifying, life-giving expression of this sacred, powerful, unifying, life-giving love is sexual intercourse. It unites the couple totally and completely —

physically, emotionally, and spiritually. To top that off, this ultimate expression of committed love has the possibility (and is bio-
logically ordered toward) the bringing about of new life. The
married couple has the incredible joy of being co-creators with
God Almighty by bringing new life into this world. Think about
that!

Of course, along with this great power comes great responsibility (Jesus said it first, not Spiderman!). The possibility of having a child as the natural result of sexual intercourse strikes fear
in the hearts of many couples. Many are not ready to have children yet, some don't want children yet, and others don't want any
more children than they already have. Thus they seek ways to still
be able to have intercourse but remove the possibility of having
children. Hence, the dreaded issue of contraception.

The culture in which we live has destroyed the notion that
human fertility is a sacred gift from God that *can* be managed in
a healthy, holy manner and not treated like a horrible, contagious
disease for which one needs to take dangerous medication, use
unhealthy devices, or have mutilating operations done to avoid
having a child. When that happens, the life-giving, truly sacred,
and unitive nature of sexual love expressed by a committed married couple is totally destroyed. And when that happens, sexual
activity becomes nothing more than mutual masturbation.

The Church has always encouraged couples to use natural
family planning (NFP) to manage their fertility in a way that
works to either avoid *or* achieve a pregnancy. When most people
hear the phrase "natural family planning," they roll their eyes and
think of it as a joke. But it's no joke. The methods of NFP that
are used today (not the old rhythm method of the days of yesteryear) are equally and in some cases more effective than artificial
contraception. NFP is a way for a couple to really learn about their
fertility, to take ownership of it, to work in conjunction with it

instead of destroying it and throwing it in the trash until they want to have kids. And here's the kicker. Among couples who practice NFP, there is a divorce rate of less than five percent. This is because NFP fosters deeper communication between couples. It challenges the couple to find other ways of being intimate and loving toward each other besides just with intercourse.

A big criticism many people level against NFP is: "Who do you think you're fooling? NFP is still geared toward not having kids, which is still contraception!" In response to that, avoiding pregnancy at certain times is a part of "responsible parenthood." Purposely cranking out as many kids as a couple can possibly have despite not having the resources to properly care for those children is not a good thing. NFP is a way of avoiding pregnancy in a manner that still respects the sacredness of fertility, remains open to life, and is still in cooperation with God, working with him as co-creators of human life.

There are no methods of contraception that are one hundred percent effective (although some are pretty close, including NFP). Barrier methods, spermicides, tubal ligation, vasectomy, birth control pills, and progestional agents all can and do fail. Besides that, the side effects of these things are horrible and in some cases can completely destroy one's fertility, eliminating the ability to ever have children. The important point in all of this, and the message that the Church is trying to get across, is to be open to life. A child is a gift from God, not the *right* of the individual. And if you are practicing responsible parenthood and still end up pregnant, then trust in the Lord. He will provide. (There are lots of good resources out there for NFP. Check them out.)

Contraception is one of many "pro-life" issues that concern human sexuality. Of course, the big pro-life issue that everybody is familiar with is that of abortion. Many pro-choice advocates no longer question whether abortion is the taking of a human life.

With the advances in medical science, operations can now be done on unborn children. Children who are born very prematurely, who in the past would not have survived, can now be taken care of and brought to full health, while many unborn children of the same stage of development are aborted (put to death). There are children who have actually survived an abortion procedure and are alive today.

The issue for many pro-choice advocates is not the moral question of abortion, but the *right* to be able to have an abortion. The pro-life response to this is what we have been saying all along: Everybody has the *"freedom"* to choose to do something morally evil. Everybody has the *"choice"* to murder, but being able to freely choose something does not make it right. True freedom cannot exist without responsibility, and choosing to end an innocent human life is certainly not an act of responsibility. It is a lethal act of ultimate irresponsibility.

There is an unbelievable amount of denial that goes on regarding abortion. When a woman is pregnant, when the man has impregnated her, *they* are going to have a child, a human being. It's not a rabbit or a turtle growing in the womb. It is their son or daughter. That is an undeniable fact! To *force* open the cervix, and violently, painfully cut apart and rip that unborn child from his or her mother's womb is without a doubt an act of murder. The other methods of abortion that are used are even more grizzly!

Having an abortion is a traumatic event that *will* (sooner or later) affect and haunt the persons involved for the rest of their lives. One can only stay in denial for so long. Many women (and men) try to rationalize and deal with the horrendous psychological aftershock of abortion in different ways. Some have more abortions as an attempt to rationalize that it's okay. Some try to have another child right away to make up for the guilt of aborting their previous child. Some go through an entire ego shift to deal with the shame and guilt.

With abortion, one must deal not only with the loss of a child, but also the loss of being a mother or father and all that goes with it. Abortion is a devastating, insidious evil. When one really understands all that is involved concerning abortion on all the different levels, it is truly sickening. As Robert Oppenheimer reflected after seeing the first test of the atomic bomb, "Now, I am become Death, the destroyer of worlds." We have done the same with abortion.

As we've seen, sexual activity has the potential to produce much good or much evil. It is a very powerful thing. It is something to be treated with the utmost respect, responsibility, care, dignity, and concern. The temptations out there are strong. They'll hit you hardest when you are at your weakest. As the old hymn says, "A mighty fortress is our God!" It's only by remaining protected by that mighty fortress that we even have a chance to defend ourselves against the power of temptation. It's only God's grace that can shield us and strengthen us in those moments of weakness. But it's also by fostering a new outlook on sexuality that we can diminish much of the disordered allure. When we truly realize the profound sacredness, holiness, and life-giving power of sexuality, many of those temptations simply fade away and are replaced by the respect and beauty that our loving God intended.

There is help out there to deal with the trauma of abortion. There is hope; there is forgiveness. Contact PROJECT RACHEL at www.hopeafterabortion.com.

CHAPTER 16

The Eternal Trout Stream

I LEFT THE COMFORTABLE CONFINES of the warm, cozy kitchen with a stomach full of hearty, hot food and my favorite coffee mug in hand. As I stepped outside into the snow-covered morning twilight, I was still questioning my sanity. The freezing temperature tightened the skin on my face like the leather on an over-inflated football. I felt quick, stabbing thrusts of bitter, cold air sneak jabbing bites onto any area of my body that was not covered by at least three layers of clothes. My piping hot coffee was quickly turning into one of those trendy chilled cappuccino drinks that you pay four bucks for at your local gourmet java shop. I peaked into the back of my van to double check all my gear, then I strapped on the seat beat, said a prayer for safe travel (which I really needed that day), and I was off.

Over the next hour and a half I continued to wonder if I had seriously lost my mind. It was freezing outside, there were several inches of ice already covering everything (including most of the roads), it was snowing with the intensity of a mini-blizzard, it was the coldest day of the coldest winter we'd had in Missouri in more than a decade, and I was going trout fishing.

The trek to my favorite trout stream took a bit longer than usual because I was traveling at a greatly reduced speed and being especially mindful to look out for icy patches. My trusty red minivan (yes, I used to drive a minivan, and I loved it!) held to the road like a great Alaskan polar bear. As I slowly eased off the highway onto the back roads, I knew the real test was about to begin.

The highways were not all that bad thanks to all the salt and plowing by road crews, but the back roads were another story. They were covered with a thick, bluish-black ice and topped off with several inches of snow, with several more on the way. I slid all over the icy runway of a road, but I kept my focus and held the steering wheel tight as I charged ahead through the thick, wet sludge. In my rearview mirror, I saw a wavy, blanketed shroud of churning white muck that my back tires were broadcasting into the air. I kept on going, hoping to God that I wouldn't get stuck. As I made a right turn onto the last and worst stretch of road, I felt my tires lose their grip as I spun out of control around the bend. With some fast compensating, I was able to steer the van around just enough to regain my footing on the very edge of the road and keep from flying into the ditch and off the side of a very steep hill. Whoa, that was close!

Just when my heart beat slowed down a bit, the same thing happened. Around the next corner I slid, coming dangerously close to the edge of my demise! With my adrenalin pumping like a crazed bull elk, I slowly eased over into the other lane and stayed in the tracks made by what appeared to be the only other vehicle that had ventured that way in the last twenty-four hours. Ever so cautiously, I crept down the last few hundred yards and then thankfully came to a stop as I parked in the small lot next to the river access trail.

The snow was still coming down fast and hard. I took a moment to catch my breath, and then I hopped out into the savage winter day to begin my fun! As I put on several more layers of clothes and readied my fishing gear, my heart began to race once again, but this time it was racing with the excitement of hooking into a hungry, hearty, winter trout! Down the hill I raced with the snow blasting me in the face so hard that it was difficult to see what exactly lay ahead.

As I looked around, it was obvious that I was the only guy crazy enough to do this sort of thing. But I didn't care. The snow was truly virginal, with only deer and rabbit tracks to join my own. It was absolutely spectacular! The pure white of the surrounding snow-covered woodlands was visually interrupted only by the slender burnt umber of tree trunks and cedars peaking through the all-encompassing wall of frozen flakes. Even if I were on some kind of reality-numbing hallucinogenic drug (which I've never taken and certainly don't recommend), I doubt if I could have conjured a scene more breathtakingly beautiful and profoundly surreal.

As I marched onward to the trout-inhabited waters, the bright sunlight seemed to pulsate through the impregnated clouds as it filled each and every falling flake with a heavenly golden glow. Billions upon billions of illuminated sparkling ice crystals were falling from the sky as if it were raining diamonds upon a field of plush, billowy cotton candy. As I looked up, I saw a majestic bald eagle soaring overhead. His proudly fierce white head and tail feathers were all but invisible as he made his way through the wintry sky en route to probably fetch a trout for lunch.

When I finally made it to the river I just stood there, deep in a divine trance like I'd never before experienced. My eyes rested as they fell upon the calming steel blue of the steadily flowing trout stream, which carved its way through the surrounding desert of white. My ears delighted in hearing the soothing, gentle rush of the pure, life-giving waters. As I opened my mouth to take in a deep breath of paradise, I could taste the absolute sumptuous delight of nothingness in all its glory! Although I could feel the bitter cold on the skin of my slightly exposed face, it felt as if I were not wearing skin at all that day. At that very moment, I felt as if I'd left my earthly body behind and was now dwelling in a glorified body in the kingdom of heaven.

After standing riverside for several minutes just experiencing the phenomenon of what it means to truly exist as one of God's creations in a world created by God, I decided that I'd get to fishing. I slowly eased into the water and waded along in a memorized strategic manner, fishing all the spots that I knew would hold fish. I was fishing on autopilot as I was still spiritually, physically, and emotionally caught up in the indescribable beauty of that day. As I continued to unconsciously cast and retrieve my lure (it was too windy to fly fish), I would only be snapped out of my zone by the sudden violent attack of big, stout brown and rainbow trout. Even the fish that I was catching that day seemed to take on a new aura of unparalleled beauty. Their colors seemed to be richer, their sheen appeared shinier, and their scales seemed as if each one was highlighted by the very hand of God.

As the afternoon progressed, I continued to catch several large fish that all seemed to be controlled and driven by the Spirit that was in the air. While the daylight continued to burn, I found that catching all those fish was actually beginning to be a distraction (I never thought I'd say that!). After every cast I made, I would have to stop and knock the ice out of my line guides and defrost my reel.

I eventually sloshed out of the semi-frozen, crystal-clear water, rested my fishing rod on a tree, took off my fishing vest, and just sat on the bank, overlooking a long stretch of stream that butted up against a steep, rocky, ice-covered hill. The wind continued to blast me in the face. The snow was getting deeper by the minute. My waders were turning into a pair of ice pants. But I didn't care. I just sat there and stared at the vanishing point on the horizon where the water disappeared into the white mass of eternity. I began to wonder what might happen if I were to venture there. Would I, too, simply disappear into eternity? I wouldn't have minded.

Then it hit me. This was one of the greatest moments of my life. Something happened to me out there that words cannot describe. Something happened to me that seemed to have temporarily altered, in a profoundly sacred way, the very core of my being. It was as if the great magnitude that is the complexity of the human person was stripped away, leaving only my soul in its most purified, simplest state, to just be. To just be in the presence of God. To just be in the presence of his creation, which was now simplified by one color, one texture, one temperature, one vast arena of a holy, eternal, radiating white light. I had never felt that way, to that extreme measure, before that day, and I have never felt that way since. It was truly a taste of heaven. And you know what? I never would have experienced that taste of eternity if I had not had the courage to venture out on that journey and the faith that it would be well worth it.

Eternity! What will it be like? When will we enter into it? Who will be there? What will we do? Will we get bored? Will everything be as perfect as it is supposed to be? How good can it really be? What will we look like there? What will we talk about? What if someone we love isn't there? What if there is no place to fish or (add your favorite activity of choice)? What if there is no barbeque to eat and no frosty beverages of choice to wash it down with? What if we really don't care all that much for it? What if it just isn't what we had in mind?

Probably everybody on the face of the earth has some kind of idea of what heaven is going to be like, or should be like. And everybody's idea is probably quite different from the next person's. For some, the idea of heaven is relaxing on a picturesque sandy beach, watching the deep blue waves roll in while comfortably easing back in a heavenly lounge chair, sipping on a delicious tangy cocktail with one of those funny little umbrellas in it, and being in a state of divine calm . . . forever. For someone else, it might be casually strolling along, playing the perfect game of golf on God's personal paradise golf course with no business engagements afterward and nowhere else to be for all eternity, except right there with an endless supply of gin and tonics and St. Peter as your friendly caddy.

The things that we enjoy doing more than anything else on earth, the things that in many cases keep us going, the things that we sometimes live for, are the things that we simply can't imagine doing without in the afterlife if we are supposed to be so blissfully happy for all eternity. And more important than that, we can't imagine doing those things without certain people. How can we be truly happy if our family and friends are not there to enjoy those things with us? We could easily question the details of eternity for all eternity.

As with anything else, there are lots of books on things such as near-death experiences and personal encounters with heaven (and hell). There is also a great deal of theology written about life after death, and there are great messages of hope and comfort (and gloom and doom) in Scripture regarding the afterlife, but when it's all said and done, no one knows *exactly* what it is going to be like. We won't know for absolutely certain until we get there ourselves. There are no brochures with lovely full-color pictures and a 1-800 number we can call to arrange a tour. There are no travel agents who have been there and back numerous times to tell us how phenomenal of a place it is. For now we can only imagine, to the best that our feeble minds are able, that heaven is a place so wonderful that it is far beyond even the most incredibly awesome thing we could ever possibly imagine . . . and then some!

As much as we can think about heaven and hell and try to imagine what those places are like, the big question and concern right now is what it will technically take to get there, which is *death!* Boy, that sounds grim, doesn't it? Death is something that haunts and frightens the bejeebers out of many. For others, it inspires philosophical explorations and artistic inspiration. Still for some it is actually anticipated and welcomed with open arms. Death comes for all of us sooner or later. It is indeed the great equalizer.

No matter how much we may try to prolong our lives, no matter how powerful or wealthy we may be, no matter how big of a kingdom we have built for ourselves here on earth, no matter how we may try to make ourselves look younger or heroically fight against the aging process, the reality is that the grim reaper has got his eye on all of us and will come knocking on our door sooner or later. Wow, now that's really grim!

For most people, death brings with it great sorrow and an undeniable sense of loss. When someone we love very much dies, we can't help but experience a flood of different emotions and memories. We can't help but think of how the deceased has touched our lives and has positively impacted us in so many ways. But in the face of death and the sorrow and sense of loss that comes with it, it is important not to focus purely on death itself. Death is also a time to remember and celebrate life and commend our dearly departed to the care of God as they enter eternal life.

As Christians, we believe that death is not the end, but a new beginning. Perhaps you've heard the old analogy that compares death to birth. I don't know who came up with it, but it reminds us that we begin our lives at the moment of conception and spend nine months in the "world" of our mother's womb, all that time growing, developing, and maturing. And when the time comes, we "die" to that world and are born into this one. Likewise, we spend our time here on earth growing, developing, maturing, and once again when the time comes we die to this world and then enter into the life that we have been destined for from that first moment of conception: our eternal life with God.

But as we know, that transition into eternal life can be especially painful for those who are left behind. Losing someone we love hurts. We mourn the loss of the love that person brought into our lives. We feel empty and displaced without that person. We can feel alone and abandoned. Our sense of purpose and being can be greatly disturbed when we lose someone like a parent, a child, a spouse, or a close friend. But it's also the love of that person that gives us the hope and the strength to carry on.

It's especially the love of God that gives us the hope and strength to carry on at those times. It is God who has destroyed the power of death through Christ. It is through the passion of Jesus that we experience the unending mercy of God and the forgiveness of our sins. And it is in the resurrection of Jesus that we experience the joy and the hope of eternal life with him in heaven.

In the Gospel, we hear Jesus say, "Let not your hearts be troubled; . . . In my Father's house are many rooms; . . . I will come again and will take you to myself, that where I am you may be also" (Jn 14:1-3). This statement sums up well the purpose of our lives: to be where Christ is, to share every aspect of our lives with Christ on earth, so that we may share eternal life with him in heaven. Our time here on earth is the testing ground for where we will spend eternity. Wouldn't it seem wise to include God every step of the way? We certainly don't want to be the one who, at the gates of heaven, God asks, "Now, who are you again?"

Just as the Father was present at every moment of Jesus' earthly life, so, too, he is present in ours, and it's important to acknowledge that. He is with us in our joys and our good times, and he is with us in our pain and our sorrow. He is with us in those times that seem just too good to be true, and he is with us in those times that seem like a hellish nightmare. And though we

do at times share in the suffering of Christ, it is Chris_
desires to wipe our tears away. It is God who wishes to comfort
us in our pain and sorrow and to laugh with us in our moments
of happiness.

In the face of death and the sorrow that it brings, our guiding light is the virtue of hope. We are hopeful that our beloved
departed are in that dwelling place where they will experience the
love, the joy, and the peace of God for all eternity. We are hopeful that we, too, will join them one day. Death should remind us
to live our lives in a way that focuses on this goal.

In the cold reality that is death, we shouldn't curse and angrily
shake our fist at God for taking away a loved one, but rather we
should thank God for the gift of that loved one and the blessing
of having that person in our life. For a person of faith, death is
not a matter of saying, "Goodbye." It's more like saying, "See you
later." We hope and believe that if we have lived our lives in accordance with God's will, then we will see that person again in a
much better place, where there is no more sickness and death,
where there is no more pain and suffering, where there is no more
rat race and no more hardships to endure. We look forward to
paradise eternal!

Of course, the biggest thing that gets in the way of realizing
all of this and the thing that really puts a damper on our hope in
the midst of death is the sinister, crushing power of doubt. Doubt
is that which darkens the light. It snuffs out the fire of joy and
expectation. It muffles the exalting shouts of victory. Doubt rips
away the strong hand we've been holding onto for support. It
incinerates the last bit of spiritual nourishment that has kept us
going. To put it as simply as I can, doubt destroys faith. And without faith, we are dead.

Whenever I think about the derailing devastation that comes
from doubt, I can't help but think about an experience I had back

in grade school many years ago. For your benefit, I'll share with you this humiliating tale of woe: When I was in the fourth grade, I decided that I wanted to learn how to play a musical instrument and be in the school band. I couldn't decide if I wanted to play the guitar (which I still play today) or if I wanted to play the saxophone.

After a great deal of consideration and forethought, I finally decided on the saxophone, mostly because it was shiny and had so many cool buttons and levers on it. After a long talk with my parents and promising them that I would practice every day and take great care of my instrument, they finally agreed and bought me a saxophone. And so I started taking lessons at school and eventually started playing in the beginning band. By the time sixth grade rolled around, I was still playing and doing pretty good. I was even asked to play a solo piece for the upcoming Christmas concert.

I decided that I'd play "The Little Drummer Boy" for my solo piece, so I practiced it again and again and again until I finally had it memorized to the point that I could play it in my sleep. Finally, the big day arrived for the Christmas concert and it came my turn to play. I was totally confident that I would do a good job and play my piece perfectly. But when I got up on stage with all those lights on me and everybody looking at me, I choked! I played a few notes and then went completely blank. I made another attempt to play it, but it was of no use. I was like the proverbial deer in the headlights. I froze in shock and disbelief. After I regained enough of my wits to realize it was pointless to continue, I hung my head low and walked off the stage in humiliated disgust. If that saxophone had been a guitar, I might have done a re-enactment of Jimi Hendrix at the Monterey Pop Festival and set my saxophone on fire and smashed it to bits. I was enraged by my horrible failure.

This phenomenon of completely blowing something at the last moment, something that we know we can easily do, is something that has probably happened to all of us at one time or another. It happens in sports all the time; we see an extremely talented athlete suddenly choke on what would have been a very easy game-winning point. It happens in the business world; a polished and experienced executive suddenly bombs on a very important presentation. It happens in our relationships with others; we suddenly just can't muster the gumption to say what needs to be said or do what needs to be done.

No matter what the situation, it's a terrible feeling when this sort of a thing happens. We ask ourselves again and again, "What happened? How could I have possibly messed that up?" The reason that we fail at things at that moment of truth is because we suddenly have just a hint of doubt. And that hint of doubt can quickly turn into a strong suggestion of doubt, and that strong suggestion of doubt then turns into a command of doubt and then it's all over.

We've all most likely heard that great story of Jesus walking on the water. Another part of that story that we usually don't focus on all that much is the part where Peter gets out of the boat and (at Jesus' invitation) begins to walk on the water as well. But then something happens, Peter begins to sink and Jesus has to rescue him. It's easy to imagine what's going through Peter's mind, "Holy cow, I'm actually doing it. I'm walking on water! Jesus is here, so I guess everything is going to be all right. But wait a minute, this can't be happening. I can't walk on water . . ." And thus he begins to sink. We then hear Jesus say to him, "O man of little faith, why did you doubt?" (Mt 14:31).

Doubt is something that can negatively affect us in all areas of our lives, not just at those moments when the pressure is on or in the face of death. We can begin to doubt lots of things on a daily basis. Some have doubts that their spouse really loves them. Some have doubts whether their parents really love them. Some

⌐oubt their health. Some doubt the success of their career. Some doubt their financial security. Some doubt their ability to do one thing or another. Some doubt the existence or at least the activity of God in their lives. Doubt can spread like a wildfire and eventually ruin our lives and scorch the very core of our soul.

Like Peter, when we begin to doubt, we begin to sink. Once we start sinking, it can be very easy to start to drown in our doubt. When that happens, we can lose all hope. When we lose hope, it's all over. It's vital to remember that our Lord assures us that he is with us always. He is always there reaching out to us, wanting to pull us up in those times that we are sinking down. He is always there desperately trying to fill our lives with hope and peace in the midst of those storms of life that can frighten and overwhelm us. Yet we so often fail to take his hand because we sometimes don't recognize him, just as Peter and many others did not at first recognize Jesus for who he was. But you know what? The more we begin to trust in the Lord at all times and in all things, the easier it will be to then recognize him. And the more we learn to recognize him, the easier it will be to take his hand and hear those same words he spoke to Peter, "Take heart, it is I; have no fear" (Mt 14:27).

As I stated earlier, doubt can enter every aspect of our lives, but the snow-balling effect of doubt can come to its ultimate culmination in death. When we are consumed with the sorrow and fear that comes with death, we can be lulled into a state of frozen hopelessness. When we see the casket of a loved one being lowered into the ground, the realization that we will not be seeing that person anymore here on earth is overwhelmingly real. But it is by the power of hope and with the eyes of faith that we come to realize and truly believe that it is not the end, only a new beginning. Again, it is not, "Goodbye," but only, "See you later." It is not the end of the line, just the end of a journey that takes us to our true destination.

Going back to my winter trout-fishing story, I never would have experienced that day, which was quite possibly the most beautiful day of my life, if I had not had the courage to venture out on that journey and the faith to know that it would be well worth it. The journey was very difficult. I slid off track a few times, I had second thoughts along the way, I didn't know if I was doing the right thing, but it was my faith in what was ultimately ahead that kept me going.

As we go through the journey of life we have lots of second thoughts, fears, and apprehensions along the way. We fall off the track and slip and slide time and time again. It's easy to lose our way and to feel uncertain about where that journey will take us. We can never be absolutely one hundred percent sure about anything in life (except death and taxes). But no matter how difficult and uncertain our journey may be, the important thing is to never lose hope that our final destination, the kingdom of heaven, will be well worth all the struggle and pain. If we strive to make every step along the way one that we take with God as our navigator and guide, then we have nothing to worry about.

On the other hand, if we're walking blindly through life, living only for the fleeting selfish pleasures of the day, and only including God in our journey when we use his name to curse, then you can bet that we will be robbed by the thieves of hopelessness and despair at every corner. When the glamour and sparkle of earthly treasures blind us from looking ahead to the mind-blowing beauty of eternity, we can certainly have no doubt that our lives will be full of doubt.

In the grand scheme of things, our journey of life is very short. But it is an extremely important one. The destination of our eternal dwelling depends on it. We only get one chance to get there and there's no going back. So hold on tight! Keep your hands on the wheel and your eyes on the road. Have no fear of the treacherous obstacles that lie ahead. Be very cautious, but be valiantly courageous. Never lose hope. Listen to the Almighty Navigator and follow his directions. Have faith that it will be well worth the struggles and sacrifices that come along the way. Keep on plowing ahead no matter what, and realize that the end is only a glorious new beginning!

CHAPTER 17

Bass Fishing Bonanza

IF OUR WORLD WAS LIKE a huge freshwater lake and loaded with big, hungry, largemouth bass, we'd be in a heck of a lot of trouble! Boy, oh boy, those bass can be mean rascals! They hide out in sneaky underwater haunts and pounce on all sorts of poor little critters that happen to come their way. Frogs, snakes, insects, crawdads, birds, small rodents, and fish of all kinds (including other bass) will all get pummeled, mangled, brutalized, soundly thrashed, vacuumed up, and chomped to bits if they cross the path of a hungry or even slightly temperamental largemouth.

It is, of course, that merciless, aggressive nature that makes the bass such a tough fighter and a challenging and fun fish to catch (not to mention that they're mighty good eatin'). There are lots of different ways that one can fish for bass. There are lots of different tackle and baits that one can choose from to pursue Mr. Bigmouth. There are lots of different places and conditions that one can find when fishing for largemouth bass. All these variables make the bass-fishing experience one that appeals to everybody from hardcore tournament fishermen to the recreational angler. One might say that the largemouth bass is the all-American warm water/freshwater game fish of choice.

Regarding my personal bass-fishing career, I fished for them as a kid quite a bit, but as I got older my interest in bass fishing tapered off some due to the fact that I didn't have a boat and I was losing tons of tackle trying to fish from the shore all the time. All that changed when I decided to buy a float tube. A float tube, or belly boat as they are sometimes called, is basically an inner tube with a place to sit in the middle. It's kind of like a floating easy chair with a bunch of pockets for one's tackle and gear. With the use of kick fins, one can maneuver around a body of water and access all kinds of great fishing spots that otherwise would have been impossible to get into or launch a boat. Not to mention that fishing out of a float tube keeps you cool during those hot summer days.

Believe it or not, I don't really have any epic bass-fishing stories. I have no tales of relentless desperation or unstoppable vigor regarding fishing for bass. All I can say is that I love it and it's always an occasion to simply have a great time with friends and family. I can also say that the good Lord has blessed me with some mighty big bass over the years. I've caught an eight-pounder, several six-pounders, many five-pounders, and loads of fish in the four-pound range. As with everything else in my outdoor endeavors, I do lots of experimenting, find a few things that work consistently, and use those tactics and techniques like there's no tomorrow.

When it comes to catching good-sized bass consistently, I've found that nothing does the job quite like a plastic grub, lizard, worm, or other meaty looking rubbery morsel. Whether fish are active or inactive, they just can't seem to pass up a twitching, crawling, slimy, salty, grubby looking chunk of who knows what. And even if they're not hungry, those gross-looking pieces of plastic just seem to offend their sensibilities enough to make them take a swat at it out of sheer aggravated curiosity. Of course, I like to fish crank baits, spinner baits, top water, and all the other traditional bass tackle, but to feel that "tic . . . tic . . . tic . . . WHOMP!" of a bass hitting a plastic bait is so much fun that I just have a hard time talking myself into using anything else for long periods of time.

As any dedicated bass angler will tell you, there is a lot involved in the process of catching those fish consistently. Contrary to what many non-fishing folks imagine, serious fishing (no matter what the species of fish) is not a matter of lazily plopping down on a grassy bank with a cooler of beer (or soda), a big bag of crunchy yet greasy face-stuffing snacks, a bunch of wiggly, dirty, goo-oozing night crawlers, a cheap flimsy fishing rod, and a big red bobber and then waiting all day for a hungry fish to lethargically swim by and decide to eat.

Serious fishing is much like hunting, in that one is actively pursuing one's prey. One is methodically seeking out the fish, not necessarily waiting for the fish to come to him or her. And in order to be successful, one has to do his homework. One has to know about the fish's behavior, habitat, feeding and spawning patterns, and how temperature and water clarity will affect them. One has to know about what food sources are available at different times of the year, what affect the weather will have, and so forth. It's a strategic game of hide and seek.

The one thing you can be sure of is that in trying to latch on to one of those aquatic big-mouthed buffoons, you'll be doing a lot of casting. In a good day's fishing, one will have made several hundred, if not thousands, of casts. You've got to keep at it. You've got to cast, cast again, cast some more, and just when you think you've made your last cast, you cast a few more times for good measure.

Bass fishing is a proactive (I hate that word) activity. One is constantly *doing* something. It takes a great deal of perseverance to be successful. A few chapters ago, I talked about the importance of "being" without necessarily "doing," but don't get me wrong. When there is something to be done, then by golly do it!

That's the key to bass fishing: getting out there and doing it (while having fun and relaxing, of course.)

On the spiritual level, it reminds me of the story Jesus tells in the Gospel of Luke about the "Rich Man and Lazarus" (see Lk 16:19-31). Many theologians refer to this story as "The Man Who Did Nothing." In the story, the rich man was, well, rich. He wore the finest clothes, ate the best foods and lived the high life. Meanwhile, the poor man, Lazarus, laid around the rich man's door with dogs licking his sores. Lazarus only wanted to eat the scraps that fell from the table. As the story turns out, in the afterlife their roles are reversed. Lazarus experiences joy and the rich man experiences pain and misery. The truth be told, we can't help but to feel a sense of satisfaction that perhaps both got what they deserved.

When we take a closer look at this story, we have to ask what exactly was so bad about the rich man? After all, he didn't have Lazarus arrested or hauled off. He didn't refuse to let him eat the scraps. He didn't give him a good beating while he was lying around the door to get him out of the way. He didn't cast dispersions upon Lazarus or invite his rich friends over to engage in any kind of high school level petty torment and hazing with Lazarus as their victim. He really didn't *do* anything to Lazarus. But that was the problem. He didn't *do anything*.

In the person of Lazarus, the rich man was confronted with dire human need and he didn't do anything to help. The rich man committed a grave sin of "omission," the sin of doing nothing. Several years ago, I heard a homily where the priest made the bold statement that of the people who end up going to hell, most probably get there not because of what they did, but because of what they didn't do.

In reflecting on that, I believe he's probably right. Millions of horrible, unspeakable tragedies have occurred throughout the centuries, and are still happening today, because of what others *did not* do, because *nothing* was done to stop or prevent these things from happening. I'm sure that each of us can think of terrible things that have happened to ourselves or others for the same reasons. We can all think of devastating situations where we say, "You know what, this or that wouldn't have happened if this or that *would have* been done. If only someone *would have* said something, if only someone *would have* done something."

Even on a much less tragic level, think of how much more good we could be doing for God and for others in our everyday lives by simply putting forth a little extra effort and *doing* something. We can positively impact peoples lives in ways we'd never imagined by simply making the decision to *do something*, instead of waiting for someone else or expecting someone else to do it for us.

Sometimes it really doesn't take much effort at all to do something that will have a powerfully positive impact. Perhaps it's speaking up to defend someone or to give a word of encouragement. Maybe it's taking the time to lend a helping hand or having the courage to tell someone the truth about a certain sensitive situation. "Fraternal correction," they call it. Perhaps it's setting aside some time to pray or just doing a random act of kindness for someone who could really use it. All those things can make a huge difference in someone's life.

Nike seems to have the copyright on the phrase "Just do it." But that should be our motto spiritually as well. There are lots of opportunities for us to do good every day. But no one is going to make us do those things. Most likely, no one will even suggest that we do those things. But, like the rich man in the Gospel, if we choose to do nothing in the face of sin or in the face of human need, then nothing changes for the better. And when nothing changes for the better, we can be sure that plenty of things will change for the worse.

Just like a bass fisherman has to cast and keep on casting, we have to do and keep on doing in order to bring about the kingdom of heaven here on earth. But, of course, in the process we are going to get snagged from time to time. There are going to be times that we seem to be losing all our tackle and that our efforts seem to be all in vain. There are also going to be times that we make mistakes, there are times that we will get hurt (and hurt others) in the process of striving to do good. And in order to untangle things, we have to learn to forgive.

To truly forgive is a hard thing to do. Jesus tells us, "Love your enemies, do good to those who hate you, bless those who curse you, pray for those who abuse you. To him who strikes you on the cheek, offer the other also" (Lk 6: 27-29). These are words we generally don't like to hear. This is without a doubt one of Jesus' most challenging teachings. We'd much more like to adhere to that other popular Bible verse of the Old Testament which says, "Eye for eye, tooth for tooth" (Ex 21:24, Lev 24:20, Deut 19:21).

These words that Jesus speaks in the Gospel are words that draw a great deal of criticism from non-Christians and Christians alike. We don't want to hear this message. He can't be serious. We're supposed to love people who have done terrible injustices to us and others? We're supposed to pray for those who mistreat us? I don't know about you, but when I'm mistreated, the first thing that comes to mind is usually not a prayer, or if it is, it's a prayer that they fall off a cliff or something. There's no getting around this message. Jesus means what he says. This message is the absolute embodiment of pacifism, or is it?

Whenever I hear this passage I think of those *Rocky* movies with Sylvester Stallone. It seems that in all of those movies, the grand finale is always the final boxing match with the guy who has taken away Rocky's title and has humiliated him beyond belief. And in all of those final matches, Rocky is taking another beating and it doesn't look good. But then he does something that seems insane: he offers his opponent free shots. If he gets punched on one side of the face, he offers the other side. If he gets punched in the nose, he offers a shot to the stomach as well. If he takes his opponent's seemingly hardest hit, he asks him to hit him even harder.

And the way it always turns out is that he eventually wears his opponent down to the point that he has nothing left, and then Rocky uses his last reserve of strength to finish him off and win the match. In our struggles with those who seem to be our enemy, our purpose is not to wear them out so we can then beat them to a bloody pulp and show them what for, but rather it is to actively combat hatred and mistreatment with charity and love, sometimes tough love.

There's a reason people do terrible things to others, and when we respond by doing terrible things back, we're throwing gasoline on the fire. Of course, I'm not saying that one should not seek justice in the face of criminal wrongdoings, and unfortunately sometimes it takes force to bring about peace, but when we perpetuate hatred and evil, we ultimately fail to destroy it and therefore fail to heal it with the love and mercy of God, who is the source of all forgiveness and healing.

I once heard a story of a former inmate of a Nazi concentration camp who was visiting a friend who had gone through the experience with him. His friend asked, "Have you forgiven them yet?" He answered, "No, of course not! I'm still consumed with hatred and anger for them." His friend responded, "Then they still have you in prison, don't they?" The moral of the story here is that our enemies are not always those who hate us, but often those whom *we* hate.

And when we refuse to forgive, we keep ourselves in a prison. We keep ourselves bound and chained to the injustice we've experienced. Our hurt and our pain from that experience comes to own us. It keeps us held hostage. It can dominate and ruin our lives. Healing and liberation from that pain only comes by means of forgiveness. Forgiveness brings about true and lasting peace of mind and well-being. Forgiveness heals the sense of separation between us, God, and others.

When we become willing to forgive and allow ourselves to be forgiven, we free ourselves from the bondage of an unforgiving attitude and allow God's love to flow through us unhindered. But most importantly, the primary principle in all of this is that if we expect God to forgive us of our sins, if we *want* God to forgive us of our sins (and all of us are sinners), then we *have* to forgive others. The measure in which we forgive is the measure in which God will forgive us.

Obviously, forgiving someone is not an easy thing to do. It may take us a long time to finally forgive someone of something. To top that off, we may have truly forgiven someone, but the scars and the hurt may continue to linger on and haunt us. Forgiving someone may be an exhausting ordeal. But when it's all said and done, it is an ordeal that brings healing, peace, and true liberation from the captivity of sin and hatred.

Whether it's struggling to forgive someone, trying to do good, heroically striving to avoid sin, trying to catch a trophy fish or hunt down a monster buck, or anything else in our lives, perseverance is the name of the game. We have to keep getting back up when we fall down and keep moving on. We have to continue to carry those crosses that come our way. We have to continue to seek the grace of God to keep us strong. We have to continue to strive to sanctify our lives.

To "sanctify" our lives means to make our lives holy. To be holy means to sincerely seek to live out the will of God. And as we've already discussed, the will of God ultimately is to love him, love one another, and avoid sin. When we think of "holy" people, saints, and all that good stuff, we have a tendency to envision some kind of obscure, overly pious, fanatical figure of the days of yesteryear who lived in a cave and did nothing but pray, fast, do good deeds, and the like. When we think of a saint we often think of someone who has lived out his or her life in a manner that would be absolutely impossible for us to ever achieve. The idea that we are all called to live saintly lives may seem like a hysterical joke! But it is no laughing matter. We are all called to be saintly, holy people, and very importantly, to still be ourselves in the process. God has given us each distinct personalities, senses of humor, talents, interests, and so on. God is not calling us to deny those things and to forcibly transform ourselves into someone else. As a wise old priest once told me, "Be your own man, but be a man of God!"

When one studies the lives of the saints it becomes clear that some of the greatest saints were once the greatest sinners. The difference between a saint and a sinner is that the saint never gave up trying to do better. The saint never threw in the towel when things got rough. A saint is one who never ceased getting back up when the destruction of sin knocked him flat on his face! A saint is one who humbly and honestly recognized his or her sinfulness, actively turned away from it, and then turned to God. We are challenged to do the same, but so often we justify our sinfulness by comparing it to others. We have a tendency to contrast our moral lives with those of others in order to make ourselves feel better, thus inhibiting that real need of repentance, holiness, and sanctification.

That contrasting which we sometimes do can really do a number on us. It's interesting to note how the use of contrast is such a powerful and important element of things such as music, painting, photography, and any other means of artistic expression.

In landscape painting for example, a particular tree that really isn't painted all that well can be made to look much better if everything else in the painting is done all the more poorly. In a piece of music, a badly played instrument may sound great if everything else in the piece is played exceptionally horrible. A skilled photographer can focus on something which in and of itself isn't all that photogenic and make it look spectacular by placing the subject in the midst of a really ugly or distracting background.

Contrast can also be a powerful tool in sales and marketing. If you go to a used car lot, you can end up buying a real piece of junk simply because everything else on the lot looks that much worse. We can get suckered into buying all sorts of stuff that we really don't need or that really doesn't work all that much better than something we already have simply because it was advertised to us in a way that made us think it was so much better and that life without it would be a treacherous ruination.

In one of Jesus' parables, he tells of a Pharisee and a tax collector and how each prayed in the temple (see Lk 18:914). This particular parable shows a tremendous contrast in characters. One leaves the temple justified in God's mercy, while the other leaves condemned. The Pharisee really pats himself on the back because he hasn't committed the sins that the tax collector did. While he is seemingly convinced in his own mind that he is giving glory to God, he is at the same time condemning himself by means of his pride and his failure to recognize and repent of his own sinfulness. He glorifies himself by contrasting his sins with those of the tax collector. Meanwhile, the tax collector comes before God, hangs his head low out of shame for his sins, and begs God for mercy. This man who would have been recognized publicly as a "sinner" was justified in the eyes of God because he truly had a contrite heart and was truly sorry for his sins. He didn't contrast his sins with anyone. He recognized them for what they were.

Sometimes we can become like that Pharisee. We can find ourselves focusing our attention so much on the sins of others and contrasting our sins with others so much that we fail to see the gravity of our own sins. We can get so caught up in judging others that we fail to see our own need of repentance. It can be easy for us to say, "Yeah, I may have done this or that, but look what that person has done! Now that's really bad!" We can read the newspaper each morning and see page after page of terrible crimes that people have committed and say to ourselves, "Wow, I'm not so bad after all!" Just like that Pharisee, we can attempt to justify ourselves by pointing our finger at someone or something else.

Whether we've concocted an elaborate hoax to steal ten million dollars or we simply steal ten dollars from someone, the fact of the matter is that we stole. Whether we tell a lie that destroys an entire corporation or we tell a lie to a friend or family member to get out of doing something we don't want to do, the fact is that we have lied. Although there are degrees of sinfulness, the reality is that a sin is a sin. We have no idea how one seemingly harmless little sin is going to affect our lives and our world.

Those terrible crimes we see in the newspapers all began by someone committing one seemingly harmless little sin that snowballed into something bigger. Jesus challenges us to put things in true perspective, to do away with our clever use of contrast. He challenges us to humble ourselves so that we may be exalted in God's eyes. He challenges us to point our finger at no one else and nothing else until we have first pointed it at ourselves.

Having the honesty and the humility to recognize our faults, failings and weaknesses, and then having the courage to do something about it is the first and most important step in sanctifying one's life. It's the actual doing something to make progress in those areas that becomes the ongoing, daily struggle and challenge. As St. Josemaría Escrivá so often taught, the sanctification of our lives can come about most potently through our everyday experiences, our work, and our daily activities.

As we all know, life can dish out many hardships and aggravations. The stress and frustration that enters our lives can either make us or break us. Consciously offering up that stress, frustration, aggravation, and hardship for a particular intention, as a spiritual sacrifice, is one of the most fruitful and powerful forms of prayer there is. It also brings about a sustaining sense of peace that gives us the strength to carry on. Many of the saints spent their lives offering up the pain of horrible illnesses they had or other such tribulations in order to save many souls. When we share in Jesus' suffering on the cross by offering up our own suffering, we share in the bringing about of Jesus' redemption.

It can be fairly easy to recite a few prayers here and there and think we're really doing good things for the salvation of the world (and we are), but when we are willing to make real sacrifices, and offer up real pain for the Kingdom of God, we can be sure we're having an even more powerful impact. What's more of a sacrifice: taking a few minutes to rattle off a quick prayer, or driving to and from work with the radio off in order to offer some prayerful silence to the Lord? What's more of a sacrifice: saying a prayer before a meal, or giving up that meal and fasting? And again I ask, what's more of a sacrifice: making a rushed phone call to someone who could really use the human contact, or giving up a good chunk of free time to pay that person a visit?

There are lots of things that we can do every day that can truly transform our lives into a living, prayerful, holy sacrifice to the Lord. Of course, I don't need to point out that we should not go out of our way to make our lives miserable and beat ourselves up so we have something to offer to God. There are plenty of simple, yet challenging things we can do. It's amazing how the simplest things can be so difficult to offer up to the Lord. Not putting cream or sugar in your coffee as a prayer offering to the Lord may be much more difficult than running a few miles on the treadmill for the Lord. The important thing is to be aware of the many opportunities that come our way and to make those sacrifices to the Lord, make them for the good of our world, for the good of your family, and for the good of yourself.

It is equally important to keep in mind that there are other methods of sanctifying one's life besides offering up all the difficult and challenging things that come our way. Offering God the joys, the blessings, and the fruits of our labor are just as important. Consciously praising God with those simple, satisfying, life-giving, beautiful, and joyful things that money cannot buy, and that no career can foster, can bring about a deep intimacy in our relationship with God. It helps us to realize just how much God truly loves us. It motivates us to live better, holier lives in order to nurture that loving relationship.

If you can't find anything to thank and praise the Lord for, just go spend some time in the great outdoors, in the raw manifestation of God's awesome creation! It certainly works for me. Watching the sun rise and set, letting the soothing drops of rain clean my soul, feeling the wind blow through my hair, listening to the gentle sounds of a trout stream, experiencing the rushing cool water massage my tired legs, seeing the graceful and majestic ways of a whitetail deer, hearing that magical sound of a spring gobbler, admiring the hand-painted decor of sunfish and wishing I could glide through the sky like a great blue heron are all priceless gifts of beauty that come from God. I praise God with and for that beauty.

Sharing a laugh and a smile with a friend, poking fun at our mishaps, giving a hearty pat on the back, lending a helping hand, giving a kind word, hearing my nephews and niece giggle, exchanging a firm handshake with my dad, and getting a hug from my mom are the most joyful things in the world. I praise God with and for that joy.

Catching a trophy fish, harvesting a big buck, being able to use my own two hands, being sufficient in the ways of the wild world, seeing the fruit of my labor, and having a plan come together perfectly are feelings of satisfaction that cannot be matched by anything else. I praise God for and with that satisfaction. These are the things that have sustained me in my relationship with God. These are the things God has used to fill me with his presence (besides my priestly ministry, of course.) These are the things that heal me when I become sickened by the frantic, misguided ways of the modern world. These are the things that I have and will continue to search for all my life. And these are the things that I will continue to find nestled in the handiwork of the Almighty. This is why I've been hunting for God. This is why I've been fishing for the Lord.

About the Author

REV. JOSEPH F. CLASSEN is associate pastor at St. Margaret Mary Alacoque parish in St. Louis, Missouri, and an avid hunter and fisherman. He holds a Bachelor of Arts in Philosophy from St. Louis University and a Master of Divinity from the Kenrick School of Theology.

Encounter the Sacred in Everyday Life

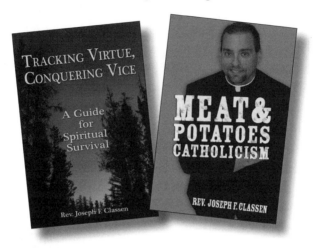

Whether it is finding God through nature or understanding the nuts and bolts of Catholicism, here are real connections and direct answers from a passionate, engaging young priest who speaks in a straight-shooting language anyone can understand.

Tracking Virtue, Conquering Vice
By Rev. Joseph F. Classen
978-1-59276-476-1 (ID# T713), paper

Meat & Potatoes Catholicism
By Rev. Joseph F. Classen
978-1-59276-335-1 (ID# T713), paper

Order your copies today at 1-800-348-2440!

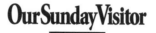

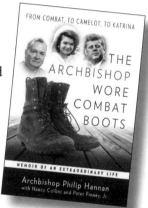

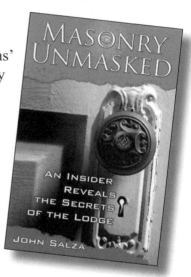